Phil Maggitti

Scottish Fold Cats

Everything About Acquisition, Care, Nutrition,
Behavior, Health Care, and Breeding

With 32 Photographs
Illustrations by Michele Earle Bridges

BARRON'S

© Copyright 1993 by Barron's Educational Series, Inc.

All inquiries should be addressed to:
Barron's Educational Series, Inc.
250 Wireless Boulevard
Hauppauge, NY 11788

International Standard Book No. 0-8120-4999-3

Library of Congress Catalog Card No. 92-36729

Library of Congress Cataloging-in-Publication Data

Maggitti, Phil.
   Scottish fold cats : everything about acquisition, care, nutrition, behavior, health care, and breeding / Phil Maggitti ; illustrations by Michele Earle Bridges.
      p.   cm. — (A complete pet owner's manual)
   Includes bibliographical references and index.
   ISBN 0-8120-4999-3
   1. Scottish fold cat.   I. Title.   II. Series.
SF449.S35M34   1993
636.8'2—dc20   92-36729
                                                       CIP

PRINTED IN HONG KONG

3456   9927   987654321

About the Author:
Phil Maggitti, a freelance writer and editor, has published nearly 250 articles about cats. He is also a former contributing editor to *Spur*, a magazine devoted to thoroughbreds and country living, and to *The Animals Agenda*, an animal-rights and ecology magazine. Mr. Maggitti and his wife, Mary Ann, bred the cat fancy's first Scottish Fold Longhair supreme grand champion.

Photo credits: Chanan: front cover, inside front cover, inside back cover, back cover (top left, bottom right), pages 9 (bottom left), 10 (bottom right), 27 (top right), 28 (top), 45, 46, 63 (top right and left, bottom left), 64; Donna J. Coss: pages 10 (top right), 27 (bottom); Larry Johnson: back cover (top right), pages 10 (bottom left, top left), 28 (bottom left and right); Mark McCullough: page 9 (top, bottom right); Carl J. Widmer: back cover (bottom left), page 63 (bottom right).

Important Note:
When you handle cats, you may sometimes get scratched or bitten. If this happens, have a doctor treat the injuries immediately.

   Make sure your cat receives all the necessary shots and dewormings, otherwise serious danger to the animal and to human health may arise. A few diseases and parasites can be communicated to humans. If your cat shows any signs of illness, you should definitely consult a veterinarian. If you are worried about your own health, see your doctor and tell him or her that you have cats.

   Some people have allergic reactions to cats. If you think you might be allergic, see your doctor before you get a cat.

   It is possible for a cat to cause damage to someone else's property and even to cause accidents. For your own protection you should make sure your insurance covers such eventualities, and you should definitely have liability insurance.

Contents

Contents

Acknowledgments

The following people helped to make this a better book: Mary Ross, who made corrections in the breed-history chapter, and who, along with her late husband, William, always believed in the Scottish Fold; Connie Webb, who read the entire manuscript, gently pointing out mistakes and tactfully making suggestions for improvement; Helgard Niewisch, DVM, who evaluated and fine-tuned the manuscript for Barron's; John C. Fyfe, DVM, C. William Nixon, PhD, and Patricia Turner, who patiently and promptly read and reread the genetics chapter, saving me from public embarrassment; Dr. Nixon and Ms. Turner also read the breed-history chapter and provided important information for it; Scarlette Zirkle, DVM, who read and corrected the chapters on reproduction and raising Scottish Folds—and then loaned me a text on theriogenology; Fred Reifsnyder, who spruced up the chapter on grooming; Karen Votava, who provided information regarding the history of the Scottish Fold; Beth Callan, VMD, who explained the intricacies of blood typing in cats; all the breeders who cared enough about their breed to send photos, even though they knew there might not be room to use every cat's photo; my wife, Mary Ann, who proofread, provided moral support and many helpful suggestions, never complained about whirring coffee grinders and clacking keyboards at 2 A.M., and who has always been such a good friend to our cats; and my two Pug dogs who sat by and under the desk, expanding their affective vocabularies, while this book was in progress.

Phil Maggitti
January, 1993

Preface

This book was written for those who want to learn about the history, personality, and day-to-day requirements of the Scottish Fold. The 12 chapters that follow explain everything a prospective Fold owner or fancier will need to know in order to select and care for a Scottish Fold.

"A Brief Chronology of Cats" outlines the circumstances of the cat's domestication and identifies the wild cats that most likely contributed to the domestic cat's development. "The Scottish Fold Story" recounts the circumstances of the Fold's discovery and development in Great Britain and its subsequent emigration to the United States.

"Acquiring a Scottish Fold," in addition to providing tips on selecting a healthy kitten, is designed to evoke an internal dialogue on the reader's part—for the best cat keepers are those who understand their motives for wanting a cat and who choose a cat that is most compatible with their habits. "Living with a Scottish Fold" provides a list of the materials you will need before you bring your new Fold home, presents hints on how to make your house cat-proof, and describes the best way to introduce your kitten or cat to its new surroundings.

"Grooming and Physical Care" reveals how often you should groom your cat, relates how you should go about doing it, and identifies the tools you will need to get the job done.

"Nutrition and Diet" tells you how much and how often you should feed your cat, what foods are acceptable, and what foods you should avoid. In "Health Care" you will learn how preventive medicine can keep your cat healthy; you will be coached in recognizing symptoms that indicate when your cat is unwell; and you will be told how to care for a sick cat.

"Understanding Scottish Folds" explores the feline psyche, which is not so mysterious as some observers would have us believe. Indeed, the more we know about the effects of evolution and domestication on feline behavior, the less we are apt to be confounded by the cat's proclivities and the better we are able to communicate with our cats.

"Cat Shows" guides the reader one step at a time through the process of locating and entering a cat show and preparing a cat for its debut. "Sexual Behavior of Cats," in addition to revealing everything you always wanted to know about feline sex but didn't know where to ask, discusses the responsibilities of breeding cats.

"Raising Scottish Folds" reviews the care a cat should receive during pregnancy, prepares the reader for delivering kittens, explains neonatal kitten development, and provides a step-by-step strategy for raising orphaned kittens.

"Scottish Fold Genetics" provides basic information about genetics and a specific discussion of the genetic peculiarities of the Scottish Fold. Finally, the back of the book contains suggestions for further reading, a list of the cat-registering associations in North America, and a list of animal-welfare associations devoted to the protection of all cats.

Whether you are thinking about buying a Scottish Fold or have just acquired one, this book can make everyday life more enjoyable for you and your cat for many years to come.

A Brief Chronology of Cats

The Cat's Family Tree

Cats belong to the mammalian, carnivorous family known as *Felidae*, whose members are exquisitely specialized and solitary hunters, feeding almost entirely on meat and almost exclusively on vertebrates. *Felidae* (or felids) can be assigned to one of three classes: Cats that can roar—the lion, tiger, leopard, snow leopard, clouded leopard, and jaguar—belong to the class *Panthera*. All nonroaring cats but the cheetah belong to the class *Felis*. The cheetah, because its claws are not fully retractable, is in a class by itself, called *Acinonyx*.

Evolution and Domestication

About fifty-four million years ago, felids began to evolve from small, tree-climbing creatures called miacids, which resembled the present-day marten. Felids with close similarities to the cats we know today did not appear until roughly twelve million years ago.

Cats were among the last animals to be domesticated. Our ancestors had gentled at least a dozen other animals—beginning with dogs, reindeer, goats, and sheep more than ten thousand years ago—before developing a relationship with cats.

Most animal behaviorists agree that cats were first domesticated in Egypt, where the earliest known pictorial representations of cats appeared in the third millennium B.C. Though some researchers do not believe that these were domesticated cats, virtually everyone concedes that cats were fully domesticated in Egypt by 1600 B.C.

Historians also disagree regarding the manner in which cats were domesticated, but we do know that cats differ from other domesticated animals in two important ways: except for the lion and the cheetah, cats live singly rather than in groups; and cats' domestication was not as closely planned or supervised as the domestication of other animals.

All carnivores are thought to have descended from a common ancestor, the miacid, that flourished about 45 million years ago. The earliest ancestors of modern-day cats did not develop as a separate phylogenetic line until the Pliocene epoch.

Indeed, some people believe that cats domesticated themselves—with scant help from humans. As an agrarian society evolved in Egypt roughly five thousand years ago, wild cats moved closer to towns and villages, attracted by discarded food and the large populations of rats and mice that thrived in granaries. When cats demonstrated their skill at policing stores of grain, farmers began feeding them to entice them to remain on the job.

The African wild cat (*Felis silvestris libyca*) is the cat that was most likely domesticated by the Egyptians. This yellow, faintly striped feline, somewhat larger than present-day house cats, is found in the deserts of Africa, Syria, Arabia, and parts of India.

Two other varieties may have contributed to the modern cat's development. Pallas' cat (*Felis manul*), a longhaired resident of Northern and Central Asia, is believed by some to be the distant ancestor of today's longhaired cats. The European wild cat (*Felis silvestris silvestris*), a forest-dwelling cat that has never been domesticated, may have bred

A Brief Chronology of Cats

The African wild cat (*Felis silvestris libyca*) is the cat most frequently mentioned as the ancestor of the domestic cat (*Felis silvestris catus*).

with domesticated cats after they had reached Europe in the fourth century.

No matter when or how the cat was domesticated, it soon became the cat's meow in Egypt. Herodotus, the father of history, observed that when Egyptians' houses caught fire, the owners were more anxious about their cats than their possessions. Upon dying, Egyptian cats were mourned, mummified, and buried in a consecrated place.

Cats were eventually exported from Egypt to other parts of the world, but the esteem they enjoyed along the Nile did not always travel with them. In China, cats were once suspected of bringing poverty into a house. In thirteenth-century Europe, cats were believed to be the familiars of witches or—worse yet—witches in cats' clothing. For the next four and a half centuries, cats were fair game for religious persecution throughout Europe. Not until the cat's reputation began to be restored during the seventeenth century was the development of an interest in different breeds of cats

possile. This interest led to the eventual creation of the cat fancy.

Development of the Cat Fancy

The cat fancy was born in London's Crystal Palace, where the first cat show was held in 1871. Harrison Weir, who organized this event and served on the panel of judges, also wrote the standards by which different breeds and varieties of cats entered in the show were evaluated. In 1887, Weir was elected president of the newly formed National Cat Club (NCC) in England. The NCC established a stud book and register, and thus began the custom of recording the ancestors of "pedigreed" cats.

The birth of the cat fancy in the United States occurred on May 8, 1895, when an Englishman named James T. Hyde organized a cat show in Madison Square Garden in New York. The following year the American Cat Club was formed for the purposes of maintaining a stud book, verifying pedigrees, sponsoring shows, and promoting the welfare of cats. Today, there are six different cat associations in North America. They register more than 80,000 cats and license 500 shows each year.

All associations register cats and license shows, publish breed standards and show rules, charter clubs, train, examine, and license judges, enforce bylaws and show rules, approve breed standards, recognize new breeds and colors, and present awards. In addition, several of the larger associations publish newsletters, magazines, and yearbooks.

Top: A handsome silver classic tabby-and-white male bred and owned by Jeanne Sprague.
Bottom left: A striking all-white female, bred and owned by Lynda and Alan Marx.
Bottom right: Liberal splashes of white generally enhance a Scottish Fold's appearance, witness this silver classic tabby-and-white male bred and owned by Bob and Linda Rader.

The Scottish Fold Story

The Early Years

Sporting a winsome, hear-no-evil expression and swing-low-sweet-chariot ears, the Scottish Fold has been blessed with a singular logo. What's more, this fetching, doe-eyed sprite has been blessed with romantic and mysterious origins.

One day in 1961 near the Scottish village of Coupar Angus, a shepherd named William Ross paused to look at a white cat playing in a neighbor's yard. The cat had caught the middle-aged shepherd's eye because her ears were folded demurely downward.

William Ross and his wife Mary were cat fanciers. They owned a seal point Siamese female, and although they did not attend shows, they bred and sold an occasional litter of Siamese kittens. When Ross told his wife about the unusual cat he had seen, Mary was intrigued. Within days William paid a visit to the neighbors who lived in the cottage adjoining the yard where he had seen the fold-eared cat playing. They were unable to provide details about the cat's origin, but they promised that if she ever had fold-eared kittens of her own, they would give the Rosses one.

"I don't have any idea how those people came to own the cat," says Mary Ross. "We gave her the name Susie. Nobody ever knew her mother, nor the father. Nor whether they had folded ears or straight ears."

About a year later Susie took up with a local tom and had a litter of two, a male and a female. Both developed folded ears. The Rosses' neighbors gave the male to some friends, who had him neutered and kept him as a pet. The Rosses got the female. She had a snow-white coat like her mother's. They named her Snooks.

Three months later Susie was killed by an automobile on the road in front of her home. "Fortunately," says Mary Ross, "Snooks was a good and prolific mother, and the Scottish Fold was launched as a breed."

When Snooks began producing kittens, the Rosses decided to do what they could to promote and perpetuate fold-eared cats. They acquired a white British Shorthair female named Lady May to breed to one of Snooks's sons. They also registered a cattery name with the Governing Council of the Cat Fancy (GCCF) in Great Britain. They chose Denisla (den-EYE-la).

After registering a cattery name, William Ross began to visit cat shows to see if anyone might be interested in cats with folded ears. A judge at one of the shows told Ross to contact Pat Turner, a Londoner with a degree from the Royal College of Art and an unyielding interest in cat breeding and genetics.

William and Mary Ross, circa 1963, with Snooks, a white, shorthaired female, their first Scottish Fold.

Top left: A sturdy, impressive, brown ticked tabby male, bred and owned by Catherine M. Symanski.
Top right: A blue mackerel tabby-and-white female, bred and owned by Gayle Johnson and Pat Wasik.
Bottom left: A red mackerel tabby-and-white male, bred and owned by Gavin and Shana Ellzey.
Bottom right: A cream-and-white van.

"The Rosses wrote to me early in 1967," Turner recalls. "At that stage they still referred to their cats as *lop-eared*, after the lop-eared rabbits. I visited them to check their cats and to bring one home with me for test mating."

When Turner returned from her visit to the Rosses, she brought home a one-year-old, white, fold-eared male named Snowdrift, who had amber-gold eyes and a short, thick tail. After Snowdrift had been installed in Turner's London home, the first female he bred was Champion Scarletina Diamond, a blue-eyed, white British Shorthair that Turner owned.

Using British Shorthairs, the straight-eared offspring of fold-eared cats, and cats with folded ears in her experimental breeding program, Turner produced 76 kittens during the next three years. Forty-two had folded ears and 34 had straight ears. She and Peter Dyte, a British geneticist with whom she conferred about her work, agreed that the gene mutation responsible for folded ears is a simple dominant. Thus, if a kitten inherits a gene for folded ears from one parent and a gene for straight ears from the other, that kitten will develop folded ears. (See Scottish Fold Genetics, page 77.)

As the Rosses had discovered already, Turner and Dyte learned that Folds' ears look normal, that is, pasted flat to the head, at birth. After 15 to 25 days, on the average, when the cartilage in normal kittens' ears is beginning to harden, causing them to stand upright, Folds' ears begin developing the crimp that produces their distinctive signature.

Turner also learned that Folds were carrying a longhair gene. Though Susie produced but one litter and both the kittens in it were shorthairs, Snooks and her descendants produced longhaired kittens. Therefore, Snooks must have been carrying a longhair gene, which she had inherited from one of her parents.

Because the gene for long hair is recessive, a cat with one gene for short hair and another for long hair will have a short coat. Such a cat has the potential to throw both shorthaired and longhaired kittens. Snooks produced longhairs when she was bred to British Shorthairs, many of which carry a longhair gene because GCCF allows breeders to cross their British Shorthairs to Persians.

In addition to her exploration of Fold genetics, Turner worked to promote the breed. She exhibited Snowdrift, who was still owned by the Rosses, in nonchampionship AOV (Any Other Variety) classes at several GCCF shows. "He was even featured on British television," she adds, "and made news stories all over the world."

Finally, Turner renamed the breed, persuading the Rosses to call their cats Folds instead of Lops because "the cartilage change in the rabbit is totally different from the Fold's." In the rabbit, Turner explains, the fold occurs "right at the base of the pinna," the visible portion of the ear that projects from the head. In the early Scottish Folds, the change occurred higher on the ear.

Ear configurations in Scottish Folds have evolved since then. In addition to the single fold in the pinna, many cats have ears with double folds. Their ears fold once at the base of the pinna, curl backward, then fold again. What's more, the ears on some present-day cats with single folds do appear more lopped than folded because the fold starts at the base of the pinna. In the early Folds —and in many pet-quality Folds today—the fold occurred higher on the ear.

The revolutions that enlivened music and hairstyles in Great Britain during the 1960s did not extend to the cat fancy, and most British Shorthair breeders were not pleased to see "their" breed used to establish the Scottish Fold. Some British fanciers also complained that the Fold was an aesthetic blunder. To be fair, British Shorthair patrons were not unique in their surliness, as many another person who has worked to develop a new breed can attest.

"People wrote all kinds of nasty articles when we first had these cats," says Mary Ross, who lost her husband in 1982 and who subsequently moved to a home for senior citizens in Scotland. "They said we were breeding deformed cats on purpose. They accused us of breeding just for the money, but we never had any profit from the cats. We were out of pocket, actually. We used our savings to keep the cats in good condition.

"The British cat fancy didn't want (the Scottish Fold)," says Ross. "At one point, someone even sent the health and welfare inspectors to our house. That's just how people are, you know."

Opponents of fold-eared cats eventually prevailed with the GCCF, which announced in *Fur & Feather* magazine that "no applications for registration or show entries may be accepted for the Lop Eared (Fold Eared) cats." (Although GCCF had registered Scottish Folds for a while, the breed was never accepted for championship competition. When Folds were shown in GCCF, they appeared in AOV [Any Other Variety] nonchampionship classes.) The reason for banishing Folds, said GCCF, was their ear configuration, which "will almost certainly lead to an increased incidence of ear disease on account of the poor natural ventilation of the ear canal and difficulty in cleaning and applying any medication."

To this day the Fold remains *felis non gratis* in GCCF, Britain's largest cat registry, even though Folds are no more prone to ear disease than is any other breed. Nor are their ears more difficult to clean or to medicate.

Equally nonsensical was the charge circulated in the British cat fancy about Folds being prone to deafness. There were several deaf Folds among the earliest members of the congregation. Their deafness, however, resulted from their being blue-eyed whites, which are subject to deafness no matter what the drift of their ears.

Not long before Folds were banned in Britain, Turner required a series of orthopedic operations and was obliged to stop breeding cats. She placed some of her Folds with people in England who were interested in working with the breed, and she arranged to have three Folds shipped to Neil Todd, PhD, a geneticist in Newtonville, Massachusetts.

Todd had learned about Folds in an article that Turner and Dyte had published in 1969 in the *Carnivore Genetics Newsletter*, which Todd edited.

Emigrating to the United States

Just before the GCCF brought the gavel down on Scottish Folds in 1971, several members of the breed emigrated to America, where they escaped the intolerance of the British cat fancy. Their march to acceptance began sometime late in 1970 when three Folds arrived at the Carnivore Genetics Research Center (CGRC) in Massachusetts, Neil Todd proprietor. The Folds sent to Todd were Denisla Joey and Judy, littermates who were born May 4, 1970, and Denisla Hester, a two-year-old Snooks daughter.

Todd had wanted the Folds because he was studying the effects of several mutations in cats. According to C. William Nixon, PhD, an associate of Todd and himself a specialist in genetics, the first litter of Scottish Folds born in this country arrived on Monday, November 30, 1971. There were two kittens in the litter: a boy named Romeo and a girl named Juliet. Both developed folded ears. The parents of these kittens were Denisla Joey

The first litter of Scottish Folds born in the United States consisted of a blue male named Romeo (above) and a female named Juliet.

and Denisla Judy, who produced a second litter the following November. Joey also produced a litter by Denisla Hester and at least one litter by a straight-eared female.

The number of Fold litters born at the Carnivore Genetics Research Center is difficult to determine. Todd, who held the cat fancy in low esteem and who refused to register his litters with any of the cat associations, did not keep the most precise records. The last Fold litter that Todd produced was born in March 1973, says Nixon, who explains that Todd had lost interest in Fold research by then.

With Nixon's help, Todd found homes for Joey and Judy, who went to live with a friend of Nixon's, where they spent the rest of their lives. Hester was given to Lynn Lamoreux, a doctoral student in genetics.

Earning Championship Status

Lamoreux did not keep Hester long. She sent the cat to Salle Wolfe Peters, a Manx breeder in southeastern Pennsylvania. Peters had begun looking for a fold-eared cat after seeing an article about Folds in the 1971 Cat Fanciers' Association Yearbook. Shortly after acquiring Hester, Peters imported two Folds from Europe, both of them males. They were named Martina Scottsman and Ackiltie Cream Charmer. Peters eventually bought another Fold, a female named Martina Shona, from Briony Sivewright, a native of Scotland who lived for a time in Utah while her husband was stationed at Hill Air Force Base.

Sivewright had imported Shona in mid-1972, after arriving in the United States. Before going to Peters, Shona produced three litters. Some of her descendants—and the descendants of the four Folds that Peters had acquired—constitute the foundation on which the breed is based in this country.

Peters's zeal inspired a tiny coterie of disciples to preach the Scottish Fold gospel in the United States. Thanks largely to Peters; Karen Votava, a

Fold breeder from Lubbock, Texas; Rosemonde Peltz, MD, a Cat Fanciers' Association board member; and others, Folds were accepted for registration—first in 1973 by the American Cat Association, the American Cat Fanciers' Association, and the Cat Fanciers' Federation, and in 1974 by the Cat Fanciers' Association. Registration status is the first step in the progression toward full championship recognition.

Peters founded the International Scottish Fold Association (ISFA) in 1974. The first co-presidents were William and Mary Ross. "Although the Scottish Fold is our national breed," wrote Mary Ross in an ISFA newsletter, "there is only one cat lover, apart from myself, actually breeding them in their native country. I wonder if any reader would like to join us?"

The answer, from the United States at least, was a reassuring yes, and Scottish Folds became eligible for championship competition in the Cat Fanciers' Association as of May 1, 1978. Acceptance was restricted to fold-eared cats only. Folds with straight ears cannot be shown in championship, but they can be registered and used for breeding.

Ironically, the Rosses' involvement with the breed had ended by this time. The intransigence of the British cat fancy and the frustration of seeing 15 years' effort go unrewarded in Great Britain led the Rosses to give up their cats. Though the sacrifices this hardworking couple had made went unappreciated in their own country, the Rosses will always be regarded as the patron saints of Scottish Folds in America.

Breeders in the United States used several shorthaired breeds in developing the Scottish Fold because mating one fold-eared cat to another often produced kittens with skeletal anomalies. Consequently, Exotic Shorthairs, a Burmese or two, and even the occasional Persians can be found among the topmost branches in the family trees of many Scottish Folds. Furthermore, when Folds obtained registration status in the United States, one association allowed breeders to outcross to Exotic

The Scottish Fold Story

Shorthairs for a brief time. Eventually, the approved outcrosses for Scottish Folds were limited to British and American shorthairs.

When the first Scottish Fold standard was written, breeders applied for recognition for shorthaired Folds only. This decision was entirely arbitrary: a triumph of practicality over pulchritude. "I advised the Rosses not to breed longhairs," says Turner, "because those that I saw had such small, tightly folded ears they looked as if they hadn't any ears at all. I thought that would only make things worse. In retrospect I'm sorry I advised that. The longhairs I've seen have been just lovely. It's so nice to see a longhaired cat that hasn't got a piggy face. And the other thing I like is that the longhairs don't have the great woolliness of undercoat you see on Persians."

Although Fold breeders made no effort to promote longhairs, no one seemed willing to take the necessary steps to eliminate them. The only way to remove an unwanted recessive like long hair from a breeding program is to spay or neuter all kittens who inherit that trait and all cats who produce it. Because Fold breeders were not unanimously willing to do this—and because some Fold breeders continued to use Persians and Exotic Shorthairs in their breeding programs even after it was no longer permissible to do so—longhaired kittens survived without sanction well into the 1980s. The longer they survived, the more likely it became that one day they would achieve championship status.

Some purists argue that only shorthaired Folds should be accepted for championship competition because Susie, the original Fold, was a shorthair. Such arguments are not waterproof. Since Snooks, Susie's daughter, carried a longhair gene, there is a 50-50 chance that she got the gene from her mother, Susie. Had Susie lived long enough to produce three or four litters of kittens with three or four shorthairs and no longhairs in each litter, one might concede that the statistical probability of Susie's being a homozygous shorthair (that is, a cat carrying two genes for short hair) was exceedingly high.

Unfortunately, Susie produced only one litter before she died. Thus, there is no way of telling whether Snooks got her longhair gene from her mother or her father. And no way for purists to prove their shorthairs-only argument on genetic grounds.

In the fall of 1986, the Scottish Fold Breed Section of The International Cat Association (TICA) voted 39 to one to accept the Scottish Fold Longhair for championship competition beginning with the 1987–88 show season. No one is certain where or by whom the first Scottish Fold Longhairs were shown in TICA, but the name most frequently mentioned in that regard is Hazel Swadberg in Renton, Washington. During 1982 and 1983, Swadberg exhibited several longhaired Folds in the household-pet classes at TICA shows in the Northwest Region. Until Swadberg decided to bring longhaired Folds to the cat fancy's attention, Fold kittens with long hair were sold, without papers, as pets. But for Swadberg's efforts, a long time might have gone by before anyone took longhaired Folds seriously, and their progress toward championship status might have been delayed.

In 1991, the Cat Fanciers' Federation (CFF) and the American Cat Fanciers Association (ACFA) accorded championship status—and somewhat different names—to Scottish Folds with long hair. CFF chose "Longhair Folds" while ACFA selected "Highland Folds." The word *Highland*, an attempted reference to the origin of the Scottish Fold, is a misnomer—and a source of amusement in Great Britain.

More than three decades have passed since Ross first noticed the fold-eared cat playing in a neighbor's yard. The descendants of that cat now constitute one of this country's most fashionable breeds. The Scottish Fold has ranked among the top ten breeds in new registrations for several years. And as though to prove that living well is, indeed, the best revenge, the Fold is now accepted in England by the newer and more forward-thinking Cat Association of Britain.

Acquiring a Scottish Fold

Preliminaries

Do you prefer a male or a female?

Some people prefer male or female cats as pets; but either sex — if given love, attention, and someone to cuddle up with at night — will make a charming companion. The cost of spaying a female cat is one third to one half more than the cost of neutering a male. Neutered males, as they get older, should not be fed a diet with a mineral composition that would produce an alkaline rather than an acidic urine. (See Nutrition and Diet, page 38.) Otherwise there is no difference in the cost associated with — or the care required in — housing an altered male or female.

Most breeders and veterinarians recommend that females be altered when they are six months old and males when they are seven to ten months old. At these ages, sexual development is nearly complete, but undesirable traits — spraying by male cats, for example — have not become habits.

Some breeders have begun altering kittens before they are 12 weeks old because a few people who buy kittens — and who sign spay-neuter agreements when they do — breed the kittens when they grow up anyway. Obviously, early neutering or spaying prevents this possibility; but it may also cause difficulties when cats grow older. As of this writing, there are no longitudinal studies demonstrating that early neutering or spaying is safe or harmless in the long run.

Cats need playmates. If you cannot afford to buy two Scottish Folds, adopt a cat from an animal shelter.

Unaltered cats are not as easy to live with as are altered cats. Whole males are wont to spray their urine to attract females and to regard any other cat as a potential mate or sparring partner. Females will come into season periodically, a condition accompanied by frequent caterwauling, restlessness, excessive attachment to their owners, occasional spraying of their urine, and an inclination to bolt out of doors within nanoseconds of their being opened.

One cat or two?

If you have no other pets and if your house is empty during the day, you should consider getting two kittens. If buying a second Scottish Fold kitten would fracture your budget, buy a straight-eared Fold kitten or adopt a kitten — one that's roughly the same age as the Fold you are purchasing — from a local shelter. Not only will you double your pleasure and double your fun by watching two kittens playing instead of one, but kittens are also less apt to be bored or lonely if they have another kitten to talk to when you are away. Of course, when you adopt a kitten from a shelter, you should follow the same guidelines you would follow when purchasing a kitten. (See A Healthy Kitten, page 19.)

A show cat or a pet?

Unless you are planning to show and breed, you want a pet-quality Scottish Fold. Pet-quality — an unfortunate and snobbish-sounding term — is used to designate cats with some cosmetic liability that argues against their breeding or showing success. Pet-quality Folds generally have ears that are not as tightly folded as a show cat's ears or a nose that is a bit too long or a muzzle that is not round enough or some other "fault" or minor constellation of faults.

If you are interested in showing but not in breeding, you should look for a show-quality Fold. Many breeders are happy to sell show-quality kittens to persons who will allow the kittens the run of the house, have them altered when they are old enough, and show them in adult classes for altered cats.

Finding a Scottish Fold

Conscientious, small-volume breeders are the best sources of Scottish Folds. Breeders advertise in cat magazines, in the classified sections of newspapers, on bulletin boards in veterinary offices, in grooming shops and feed stores, and in the yearbooks published by cat associations (see page 83). Prospective buyers also can meet Fold breeders by visiting cat shows, which are advertised in newspapers, veterinarians' offices, and cat magazines.

You may find a Scottish Fold for sale in a pet shop. If you consider buying a kitten there, ask the owner for the name of the kitten's breeder in case you have any questions about the kitten's background, food preferences, and the like.

Cost

The price of a kitten or cat is determined by quality, supply, demand, and geography. Prices start at $300 to $400 for pet-quality Folds, $500 to $600 for breeder-quality Folds, and "market price" for show cats, which begins at roughly $800.

The purchase price is not the only cost encountered in buying a kitten. New owners also have to pay for a veterinary inspection (a wise investment even if the kitten comes with a health certificate) and, perhaps, for any additional vaccinations the kitten may require. Furthermore, persons buying a Scottish Fold from breeders who live beyond driving distance must pay to have the kitten shipped by plane. Shipping costs vary with the length of the flight, the method of shipping, and the airline involved. Kittens can be shipped on short flights for $30 to $40. Transcontinental journeys can cost $100 or more.

The buyer also must pay for the carrier in which the kitten is shipped. Carriers that meet airline specifications can be purchased at cat shows, pet shops, or some airline cargo offices. A secure, durable carrier costs $25 to $35, depending on its size.

The Scottish Fold Breed Standard

All cats and kittens competing in a show—and all kittens purported to be show prospects—are judged according to written standards for their breeds. A standard is part blueprint because it describes the ideal specimen in a breed and part constitution because it is drawn up by breeders, approved by cat-registering associations, and is subject to being amended by breeders from time to time.

The following Scottish Fold standard is a composite drawn from the standards currently approved by the six North American cat registries, all of which recognize the shorthaired Fold. The standard for the Scottish Fold Longhair, which is recognized by three federations, differs from the shorthair standard in its coat-length description only.

Head: well rounded with firm chin and jaw. Whisker pads (fleshy areas on the sides of the muzzle) are well rounded also. The neck is short.

Eyes: wide open with a sweet, innocent, somewhat surprised-looking expression. Large and well rounded, the eyes are separated by at least the width of an eye. Eye color: brilliant gold to copper in most cats, blue in some white cats, green or blue-green in chinchilla and shaded silver cats.

Nose: short, broad, and gently curved. A brief stop (or subtle angulation in the skull above the nose leather) is permitted, but a definite break (or indentation in the skull) is considered a fault.

Ears: folded forward and downward; rounded at the tips and fitting snugly into the rounded con-

Acquiring a Scottish Fold

tour of the head. Small, tightly folded ears preferred over large, loosely folded ones.

Body: medium, rounded, and well padded, with medium bone. Five toes in front and four behind. Females may be slightly smaller than males.

Tail: medium to long, in proportion to the body. Tail is flexible and tapering. Longer, tapering tail preferred.

Coat: *Shorthaired Folds*: short to medium short, dense, plush, soft in texture, and full of life. Standing out from the body; not flat or close lying.

Longhaired Folds: semilong, soft, full of life, and standing away from the body. A ruff on the chest and britches on the hindquarters are desirable.

The Scottish Fold Personality

There are more than 40 cat breeds accepted for championship competition in North America. Obviously, each breed does not have a unique personality distinct from every other breed. Indeed, feline personality is more a function of body type than breed. The willowy Siamese, for example, is the most active, vocal—and some would say intelligent—cat. Siamese share these traits to a varying extent with other svelte, tubular breeds such as the Balinese, Abyssinian, Cornish Rex, and Oriental Shorthair. At the other end of the personality scale, the Persian is the most easygoing cat. It shares this serenity with other chockablock cats like the British Shorthair, the Sacred Cat of Burma, and the Exotic Shorthair. In the middle of the stream for body type and personality is the pedigreed American Shorthair.

The Scottish Fold, an amalgam of other breeds, draws the heritable part of its personality from those breeds: the British and American shorthairs, principally, with a touch of Exotic Shorthair and Persian introduced, legally until 1977, and on the sly thereafter. None of these breeds is especially active. All are placid and calm and, with the possible exception of the British Shorthair, usually agreeable to extended handling. Thus, the Fold has evolved as a sweet-tempered cat: devoted but not demanding; bouncy on occasion, but never too boisterous; more likely to charm than to challenge; displaying a British sense of decorum leavened by an American sense of self-confidence.

Although temperament is heritable to some degree, the way a kitten is raised is more important in shaping its personality. Folds that are not handled often enough between the ages of three and fourteen weeks are less likely to develop into well-adjusted family members than kittens that receive frequent handling and attention. Therefore, it is well to ask how many litters a breeder produces each year and how many other litters he or she was raising when the kitten you are interested in was growing up. A breeder who produces more than five litters a year—or who was raising three or four other litters while your kitten's litter was maturing—may not have had time to socialize every kitten in those litters properly. A breeder who raises one or two litters at a time has more opportunity to give each of those kittens the individual attention it deserves. In general, the smaller the cattery, the more user-friendly the kittens it will produce.

Basic Personality Tests

To take the measure of a kitten's personality, simply wiggle a few fingers along the floor about six inches in front of it, or wave a small toy back and forth about the same distance away. Does the kitten rush to investigate? Does it back away in fright? Or does it disappear under the nearest sofa?

Well-adjusted, healthy kittens are curious about fingers, toys, and anything else that moves within sight. Nervous or timid kittens, or those that are not feeling well, are more cautious. Poorly adjusted kittens take cover under the nearest chair.

Acquiring a Scottish Fold

The feline personality, which ranges from scintillating to shy, often is revealed in a kitten's response to an invitation to play.

If you have other pets or children at home, the inquisitive, hey-look-me-over kitten is the best choice. The cautious kitten might well make a fine companion, too; but it may take longer to adjust, and is, perhaps, better left for experienced cat owners who currently are without pets or young children. And the little one under the chair? Shy kittens need love also. Plenty of it. If you have no other pets or if you plan to acquire two kittens at once and if you have the time and patience required to nurture such a reluctant violet, God bless you. If not, perhaps the next person who comes along will be the right owner for this needful kitten.

A Healthy Kitten

A healthy kitten's eyes are bright, glistening, and clear. Its nose is cool and slightly damp. Its gums are neither pale nor inflamed. Its ears are free of wax or dirt. Its body is soft and smooth, perhaps a little lean, but not skinny. Its coat is shiny and free of bald patches, scabs, or tiny specks of black dirt. The area around its tail is free of dirt or discoloration.

A kitten with teary eyes may be in poor health—especially if its nose is dry or if it feels warm. Inflammed gums may indicate gingivitis; a kitten with pale gums may be anemic. If its ears are waxy inside, that simply may be a sign of neglect; but if they exhibit caked-on dirt, the kitten may have ear mites. If a kitten's ribs are sticking out or if it is pot-bellied, it may be undernourished or it may have worms. A kitten with a dull-looking coat or one dotted with scabs, tiny specks of dirt, or bald spots may have ringworm, fungus, or fleas. A kitten with wet hindquarters may develop urine scalding; if they are dirty, it may have diarrhea. Both urine scalding and diarrhea are signs of potential poor health.

Scottish Fold kittens have a one-in-three chance of developing osteodystrophy if both their parents have folded ears (See Fold-to-Fold Breeding, page 79). Persons considering a Fold kitten should make certain before signing any checks or contracts that one of the kitten's parents was a straight-eared cat. Prospective buyers also should make certain that a kitten has a flexible tail that is not blunt at the tip or noticeably short in proportion to the kitten's body.

Finally, when you select a kitten, ask the breeder how that kitten behaves when being groomed, how frequently it has been groomed, and what sort of comb or brush the breeder uses with the kitten. If you go to the breeder's house to take delivery on your kitten, ask for a grooming demonstration. (See Grooming Tools, page 32)

How Old Is Old Enough?

Kittenhood is one of the special joys of cat owning. Cats are cats their entire lives, but they are kittens for only a few precious months, and new owners are eager to take their kittens home as soon as possible. Nevertheless, responsible breeders do not let kittens go until they are 12 weeks old. By that age, a kitten has been weaned properly, has been eating solid food for several weeks, and has begun to make the transition to adulthood. Furthermore, a 12-week-old kitten has had most, if not all, of its distemper-series vaccinations.

Kittens that are six to ten weeks old are still babies. Take them away from their mothers and their siblings at that age, and the stress of adjusting to new surroundings may cause them to become sick, to disregard their litter training, or to "nurse" on blankets or sofa cushions—a habit they sometimes keep the rest of their lives. No matter how tempting an eight-week-old kitten might be, it will adjust better if it is allowed to remain in its original home until it is 12 weeks old.

Unfortunately, some breeders are eager to place kittens as quickly as possible, especially those breeders who have many kittens underfoot. Do not let an irresponsible breeder talk you into taking a kitten that is too young.

Buying a Show Cat

Persons interested in buying a show cat and in breeding their own cats should start with the best quality female they can find. They also should remember that quality is not always proportionate to price and that registration papers merely indicate that a cat is eligible to be registered, not that it is good enough to be shown. Any registered cat can be entered in a show, but there is a qualitative difference between a cat that can be shown and a show cat. The former is costume jewelry, the latter is a genuine pearl—often of great price.

Novices are at an even greater disadvantage evaluating a cat's show potential than they are when gauging its personality and general state of health. A runny eye is a runny eye to most observers, but eyes of the proper size, shape, and setting are more difficult for newcomers to identify. And the difficulty is compounded because kittens have yet to finish maturing.

That is why a journey of hundreds of dollars (or more) must begin with a few simple steps: visit shows, talk to Scottish Fold breeders, watch Fold classes being judged, and learn what winning Folds look like. Talk to judges when they have finished judging and ask them to recommend one or two Fold breeders. If possible, visit several Fold breeders who are willing to spend an afternoon or evening "showing" their cats at home.

Most important, study the Scottish Fold breed standard (see page 17). Take a copy of the standard along when you go to look at kittens, and ask breeders to point out where a kitten or a cat meets the standard and where it does not. If the breeder does not object, take an experienced breeder along when you go to look at kittens.

Because breeders with the best available kittens will not always live within driving distance, you may have nothing more to base an informed decision on than a few pictures and the breeder's evaluation. If the pictures are unclear, ask to see more. If you have any reason to doubt the breeder's word, find another breeder. In any case, ask the breeder to say, preferably in writing, where a kitten measures up to the standard and where it falls short. Breeders usually will not guarantee a kitten's performance in the show ring. As a Clint Eastwood character once said, "If you want a guarantee, buy a toaster." But a breeder should be willing to say whether a kitten looks like best-in-show material or a top-ten finalist and roughly how many shows the kitten will take, after it grows up, to earn the titles offered by the various cat associations.

Anyone buying a show cat is also buying the constellation of genes that cat has inherited from its ancestors. The names and titles of the first four or five generations of ancestors are recorded on a cat's pedigree. Buyers should study a pedigree to see what titles the members of a kitten's family have won—especially its parents and grandparents, for the first two generations have the greatest impact on a kitten's development.

Acquiring a Scottish Fold

The most significant title awarded in the show ring is that of grand champion. The more grand champions present in the first two or three generations of a kitten's pedigree, the better its ancestors have done in competition, and the better its chances, theoretically at least, of carrying on the family tradition.

Although some kittens never look anything but promising from an early age, the average youngster goes through several stages while it is growing up—from ugly duckling to swan and sometimes vice versa. Buyers should wait, therefore, until a potential show-quality kitten is five or six months old before buying it. A five- or six-month-old kitten is less subject to change without notice than is a younger kitten. Buyers are wise to wait until a show kitten has reached that age and, perhaps, has been shown a time or two.

Papers and Contracts

Breeders should provide a sales contract when selling a kitten. Most contracts specify the price of the kitten, the amount of the deposit required to hold the kitten, if any, when the balance of the payment is due, and so on. Contracts may also specify that if at any time the buyer no longer can keep the kitten—or no longer wishes to keep it—the breeder must be given an opportunity to buy the kitten back at the going rate for kittens or cats at that time. (A contract that specified that the breeder be allowed to buy the kitten back at the original price most likely would not hold up if challenged.) Finally, a contract should specify that the new owner has a definite period of time, usually three to five working days, in which to take a kitten to a veterinarian for an examination. If the vet discovers any preexisting conditions such as leukemia or feline infectious peritonitis, the buyer should have the right to return the kitten at the seller's expense and to have the purchase price refunded.

When buyers give a breeder a deposit on a kitten, they should write "deposit for thus-and-such kitten" on the memo line of the check. They should make a similar notation when writing a check for the balance of the payment. Buyers should be given receipts for all payments, and they should find out in advance—and in writing if they wish—whether a deposit is refundable should they decide not to take the kitten. Buyers also should remember that once a breeder has accepted money or some other consideration in return for reserving a kitten, they have entered into an option contract; and the breeder cannot legally revoke or renegotiate the offer—as some breeders may try to do—if the kitten turns out to be much better than the breeder had anticipated.

Buyers should read a contract meticulously before signing it because contracts are legally binding once they have been signed by both parties. If a contract contains any stipulations that buyers do not understand or do not wish to agree to—like a stipulation saying that the cat can never be declawed—they should discuss these issues with the breeder before signing.

In addition to the pedigree, new owners may receive "papers" when they buy a pedigreed cat. These papers usually consist of a registration slip that the new owners fill out and send—along with the appropriate $6 or $7 fee—to the administrative office of the association in which that kitten's litter has been registered. The association then returns a certificate of ownership to the new owners.

Persons buying a cat or kitten that already has been registered by its breeder will receive an owner's certificate. There is a transfer-of-ownership section on the back of that certificate that must be signed by the breeder and the new owner. Once the required signatures are present, the new owner mails the certificate, with the appropriate transfer fee, to the administrative office of the association in which the cat has been registered. The association will send back a new, amended certificate of ownership to the new owner(s).

Acquiring a Scottish Fold

Many breeders do not supply a registration slip to anyone buying a pet-quality kitten until they receive proof that the kitten has been neutered or spayed, and some breeders do not supply registration slips on pet-quality kittens at all. Breeders withhold papers to prevent unethical persons from buying a kitten at a pet price and then breeding it and to deter the use of pet-quality kittens in breedings that have virtually no chance of promoting the aesthetic advancement of a breed.

Health Certificates

Health records and vaccination certificates are the most important documents that accompany a kitten to its new home. Do not accept a kitten without these papers. Some breeders, especially those that produce a large volume of kittens, like to save money by giving vaccinations themselves. There is nothing illegal about this practice, yet there is more to immunizing a kitten than drawing vaccine into a syringe and pushing the plunger. Few, if any, breeders are capable of examining kittens as thoroughly as a veterinarian can before administering vaccinations. This examination is important because vaccine given to a sick kitten will do more harm than good. Thus, a kitten should be seen by a veterinarian at least once before it is sold, preferably before its first vaccination. Finally, all kittens being shipped by air should be accompanied by a health certificate issued by a veterinarian and by a certificate verifying that a kitten has received its rabies shot if such is required by the state in which the buyer resides.

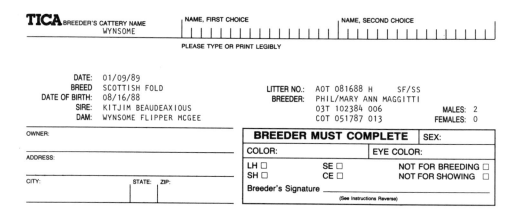

The registration (or blue) slip should accompany all pedigreed kitten sales, and all registration slips should provide breeders with the option of marking the "not for breeding" and "not for showing" boxes.

Living With a Scottish Fold

A Shopping List for New Owners

Litter pan: Some litter pans are open, some are enclosed, and some are outfitted with raised, detachable rims. The last two designs help to keep the litter in the pan when cats begin digging. No matter what the style, pans should be at least 19 inches (48 cm) by 15 inches (38 cm) by 4 inches (10 cm) deep and should be made of sturdy, washable material.

Litter: Although most litter is absorbent, none is entirely dust free. The finer the grains of litter, the more they get scattered on the floor, especially if the pan is not enclosed or fitted with a detachable rim. Deodorant litter, although frequently more expensive, is not always worth the extra cost.

Litter scoop: The sturdier the better. Always have a spare on hand.

Litter pan liners: Liners are not always practical at home because cats frequently poke holes in them, but are convenient for bundling up the contents of the pan and discarding them during motel stays.

Food and water dishes: Reusable plastic can retain odors even if washed carefully. Disposable plastic is a burden on the environment. Glass, ceramic, or metal is best. All plates and bowls should be solid and heavy enough not to tip over easily. If made of glass, they should be sturdy enough not to break, crack, or chip if a cat knocks them over.

Place mats: Whether decorator vinyl or plain rubber, place mats will protect the floor underneath food and water bowls.

Scratching post: This spares the furniture while providing cats with an outlet for exercising their natural instinct to scratch. The post should be well anchored, so it will not tip over when used, and tall enough so that adult cats can stretch while scratching. The scratching surface should be made of strong, resilient material like sisal or hemp. Floor-to-ceiling posts with shelves for cats to sit on should be especially well anchored and secure.

Center and left: Scratching posts should be covered with strong, resilient material like sisal or hemp. Right: Cat furniture provides cats with the comfort they seek at nap time.

Padded window perches: Recommended for rooms that do not have windows deep enough for a cat to sit in, perches can be clamped easily to the wall.

Grooming tools: Though cats are naturally fastidious, supplementary grooming by their owners should be part of all cats' routines. Pet shops, many veterinary offices, and vendors at cat shows carry shampoos, nail clippers, brushes, combs, powders, ointments, and sprays for your cat. (See Grooming Tools, page 32.)

Toys: A brilliant array of cat toys, all of them contrived to afford endless hours of fun, is available at pet stores and cat shows. Yet fun is not the sole criterion used in selecting toys for a cat. They must be safe as well. Balls with bells inside should be sturdy enough so a cat cannot get the bell out and swallow it. Eyes, noses, and appendages on small stuffed mice and other creatures should be virtually welded on for the same reason—as should streamers and any other attachments on toys. Before buying a toy for your cat, try to imagine how the toy could cause harm. If there is any chance that it could, do not buy it.

For all their appeal, store-bought toys are not the only shows in town. Cats will amuse themselves gladly with a crumpled piece of paper, an empty film canister, a cardboard box turned upside down with holes cut at either end, or a plain, paper grocery bag.

The same cautions expressed about store-bought toys apply to the homemade kind. They should not have dangling strings for cats to get tangled up in or to swallow, bits or pieces that cats can chew off and eat, or sharp edges on which cats could hurt themselves. Always avoid cellophane, plastic wrap, aluminum foil, twist ties from sandwich and garbage bags, rubber bands, and cotton swabs.

Beds: Even when cats are given elaborate beds, they often choose to sleep in a favorite window, on a comfortable chair, or on their owners'

Cats will amuse themselves gladly with a crumpled piece of paper and a grocery bag.

pillows. Before buying a cat bed, wait until your cat has chosen a spot to sleep in, then buy a bed to fit that spot and make it more comfortable.

Cat carrier: You will need a safe, sturdy carrier to bring your cat home in for the first time, to take your cat to the veterinarian's for checkups, and, perhaps, for vacations and travel. A good carrier, besides having a secure handle and door latch, should be well ventilated and washable. Heavy-molded plastic carriers are the best choice. They can be purchased at pet shops, cat shows, and some airline cargo offices.

Food: Most supermarkets or feed stores carry a plentiful choice of foods to suit a cat's palate and nutritional needs. The food you select should provide 100-percent-complete nutrition for the appropriate stage or for all stages of your cat's life —and should say so on the label. Products not meeting these requirements usually are identified as suitable for intermittent or supplemental use only. (See Nutrition and Diet, page 38.)

Cat-proofing Your House

Scottish Fold kittens combine a two-year-old's sense of curiosity with a teenager's athletic ability. Thus, if there are rooms you do not want your cat to investigate, keep the doors to those rooms closed. If there are fragile objects in the rooms your cat is allowed to visit, put them out of reach. Make sure all balconies are enclosed, all window screens are secured, and all electrical cords are intact. If your cat or kitten begins teething on electrical cords, wrap them in heavy tape or cover them with plastic tubes, which you can buy in an auto-supply shop. If necessary, unplug all appliances that are not in use until you are certain your cat has not developed a taste for electrical cords. To keep your cat from getting a charge out of electrical sockets, cover them with plastic plug-in socket guards, which you can buy at the hardware store.

Living With a Scottish Fold

Keep all kitchen and bathroom cleansers, chemicals, cleaners, and toilet articles in cabinets that can be closed or locked securely. Keep the lids on all trash receptacles tightly closed. Consider replacing trash containers whose swing-open lids could be dislodged if your cat overturns the containers. (Another lid to keep down is the toilet seat lid.)

When closing any door in your house—the front door, back door, refrigerator door, closet door, the door on the clothes washer or dryer—be sure your cat is not on the wrong side. Keep the bathroom door closed when you are filling the tub. When cleaning, rinse all cleansers and chemicals thoroughly from any surfaces a cat could walk on. What gets on a cat's paws usually winds up in its stomach.

Put sewing supplies and yarn away when you are finished using them. Do not leave rubber bands, hot irons, cigarettes, plastic bags, or pieces

The proper way to hold a cat: one hand under the rib cage just behind the front legs, the other hand under the cat's bottom.

of string or yarn lying around. Learn to think like a cat. Look for any potential accident—tinsel on a Christmas tree, a dangling tablecloth, a hot burner on the stove—waiting for a cat to make it happen.

Finally, keep poisonous plants out of reach. Poinsettia, philodendron, caladium, dieffenbachia, English ivy, hydrangea, Jerusalem cherry, mistletoe, and holly are some of the plants poisonous to cats. Ask your veterinarian for a complete list.

Welcoming the Newcomer

You have bought every item on your shopping list and a few extra toys as well. You have washed the litter pan, filled it with 1½ to 2 inches (3.8-5 cm) of litter, and placed it in a quiet location away from

The cat-proof house does not harbor disasters waiting for a cat to sail in and make them happen. How would you cat-proof the space above?

places where your cat is going to eat or sleep. You have made a final safety check of the house. It is time to bring your new Scottish Fold home.

If you work during the week, schedule homecoming for the start of a weekend or holiday; and remember that even though you have planned carefully for this day, it will come as a surprise to your cat—and as a major surprise to a kitten. Your Scottish Fold will be leaving its mother, playmates, and people, and the only home it has ever known. Some kittens adjust swimmingly. After they are taken from their carriers and placed in their new litter pans, they look around as if to say, "Swell place. Got anything to eat?"

Other Folds are not so self-assured. Do not be surprised or insulted if the newcomer looks apprehensive at first or looks around and scurries under the sofa. Take a chair and have a cup of coffee. Watch television or read the newspaper. The calm sounds will have a calming effect on your cat, and eventually its curiosity will take over. No cat ever has refused permanently to come out from under a sofa. Once your cat has taken the measure of the underside of the chair, it will be ready to take the measure of additional parts of your house. You will have plenty of time to get acquainted then.

A cat will feel more comfortable in its new home if something from its former home is on hand: a favorite toy, a blanket or bed, a favored food, even a small amount of soiled litter scattered in its new pan. These items give off familiar, comforting smells that are reassuring in a strange, new world.

Litter Training

As soon as you bring your Scottish Fold home, take it out of its carrier and place the cat in the litter pan. Always keep the pan in the same quiet, easy-to-reach place. For the first few days, place your cat in the pan after meals, naps, and spirited play to reinforce its instincts. Praise your cat quietly after it has used the pan. Do not allow it to wander far from the litter pan room unless you are along to supervise. If you leave your cat home alone, confine your pet to the pan room.

If your cat makes a mistake, clean the spot with a nonammonia-based, disinfectant cleaner, then sprinkle a bit of white vinegar and salt on the spot to remove the odor. A cat's attention span is roughly 20 seconds. You will not be teaching it a lesson if you drag your pet to the scene of the crime and scold it. This will only teach the cat that humans behave strangely at times.

Should you catch your cat misbehaving, a stern, disapproving *No!* will convey your displeasure. When your cat is finished, carry it gently to the pan and place your pet inside to remind it that this is where to do business. If accidents are repeated, perhaps the litter pan is too remote for your cat's convenience—there should be at least one pan on every story of the house to which a cat has access—or perhaps the pan is located too close to the places where your cat eats and sleeps.

Dirty pans also cause accidents. All waste should be scooped out of the pan and disposed of each day. Additional litter should be added as required. Once a week—or sooner if your nose suggests—dump all the litter, wash the pan thoroughly with a mild, nonammonia-based cleaner, rinse well, and put 1 to 2 inches (2.5-5 cm) of fresh litter in the pan.

If your cat is comfortable with one kind of litter, stick with that brand. Cats are creatures of habit as well as cleanliness. Switching litter may upset your cat's routine, which might result in accidents.

Top left: What's in a name? Knikear Bockear, bred by Bill and Patti Brubaker, owned by Pat and Karin Klimack.
Top right: This silver classic tabby-and-white exhibits the stout contrast sought between stripes and ground color.
Bottom: A red mackerel tabby-and-white, straight ear, bred by Thomas and Mary Van Sistine, speaks volumes about the role of fine straight ears in Fold breeding.

Living With a Scottish Fold

Introducing Children

Children who are too young or immature to treat a cat properly can pose a threat to the cat's sense of confidence and safety. Children must be mature enough to understand that cats do not like to be disturbed when they are eating or sleeping, that there is a right way to hold a cat, that cats are not toys to be lugged around the house, and that a litter pan is not a sandbox. This is why parents with toddlers should wait until their children are roughly four years old before buying a cat or kitten.

Breeders often want to meet the buyers' children before agreeing to sell a kitten or cat. Conversely, buyers with children might do best to seek breeders whose kittens have been raised with youngsters underfoot.

Children do not always understand that what is fun for them may be painful for a cat. Explain that they must be careful to watch where they walk and run when the cat is around. Explain, too, that cats often are frightened by loud, unfamiliar sounds. Ask the children to speak and play quietly until the cat gets used to them. Caution them not to pick the cat up until you feel your pet is comfortable enough in its new surroundings not to be traumatized by an impromptu ride. Teach children the proper way to hold a cat: one hand under the cat's rib cage just behind the front legs, the other hand under the cat's bottom, with the cat's face pointing away from theirs. Have them practice this while sitting down in case they drop the cat or it jumps from their arms. Reinforce your good advice with good example. If you discipline a cat by striking it, your children will, too.

Top: The exceptional uniformity of this litter is a goal for which all breeders should strive.
Bottom left: A fine straight-eared female.
Bottom right: His-and-her Folds. A male, standing, and a female sitting. Both were bred by Karen Votava and are owned by Florence Marcorelle and Marilyn Conde.

Cats can inspire a sense of responsibility in children, but children never should be forced to take care of animals. And even when a child is a cooperative caregiver, parents should keep an unobtrusive eye on the cat's feeding schedule, litter pan, and general condition. Parents should remember also that when they buy kittens for their youngsters, they buy the kittens for themselves. Inevitably, even the most cat-responsible teenagers grow up and leave home, and they do not always take their cats with them, especially when they go off to college.

Introducing Other Pets

You also should be cautious when introducing a Scottish Fold to other four-legged members of the family. The chances of hostilities breaking out vary with the age and tenure of the cat or dog already in residence. If you have an eight-year-old pet that always has been an only child, you probably should not get a new cat or kitten. If your pet is four years old or younger, you should be able to introduce a new cat if you manage the introduction carefully—and if you keep in mind how you would feel if a stranger suddenly was brought to your house for an indefinite stay.

Again, bring the new cat home on a weekend or holiday. Before you do, prepare a room where the newcomer will spend some time in isolation. Do not select the old cat's favorite sanctuary or resting place for this purpose. The idea is to fit the new cat into the old cat's routine, not to make the old cat feel dethroned.

Solitary confinement is recommended for the new cat no matter how current the old cat's vaccinations are or how well the new cat passed its veterinary test. Until you are satisfied that the new cat is not harboring any contagions that did not show up during the vet inspection—that is, for ten days to two weeks—it should have no direct and prolonged contact with the old cat. Your new pet should, of course, have plenty of visits from you, and you should disinfect your hands thoroughly after each visit.

For the first few days allow the cats to sniff, and perhaps hiss, at each other from either side of a closed door. When you feel the time is right—and after you have clipped both cats' claws—put the new cat into the cat carrier, open the door to its room, and allow the old cat to come in for a ten-minute visit. Be sure to take up the new cat's water bowl, food dish, and litter pan first in case it is carrying an infectious disease.

Repeat these daily visits until any hissing, growling, or back arching subsides, then bring the old cat into the isolation ward, but do not confine the new cat beforehand. Put the old cat on the floor and retire to a neutral corner, but have a blanket, a broom, and a pan of cold water or a fully automatic water gun handy. If the rare, life-threatening fight erupts, use the pan of water, the gun, and/or the broom to separate the cats, and throw the blanket over the nearest one. While the cat is wriggling around underneath the blanket, pick it up and return it to its original territory.

After a day or so, reinstate the brief visitations. A few days after that, attempt the free-range introduction again. Do not fret if the cats refuse to curl up together. The best they may achieve is a distant but tolerant relationship that will allow them to coexist while you go about your normal routine.

The rules for introducing a cat to a resident dog are much the same. Putting a lead on the dog will make separating them easier, if necessary. Do not remove the lead until you are sure the participants will not start fighting like cats and dogs. Be especially careful if you have a terrier, a sight hound, a retriever, or any dog that might consider the cat fair game.

Traveling with Your Cat

If your Fold complains all the way to the vet or throws up or eliminates within five minutes of leaving home, neither of you will enjoy a six-hour ride to your vacation retreat. There are pills, given about a half hour before departure, that settle a cat's stomach. Its intestines are another matter. If you must travel with a nervous cat, always travel with a roll of paper towels, some plastic baggies, and a nonammonia-based spray cleanser. And never allow your cat to ride loose in the car.

For journeys of more than three or four hours, tape a small litter pan containing a small amount of litter to the floor inside the carrier. Cover the rest of the carrier floor with a towel or disposable diaper.

If there is room in your vehicle, your cat will be more comfortable in a small wire crate roughly 20 inches (51 cm) by 24 inches (61 cm) by 21 inches (53 cm) high. A crate this size will accommodate a small litter pan and allow your cat to move around a bit. Drape a sun-reflecting blanket, which you can buy at an Army-Navy store, over the crate.

Air travel is even more challenging than car travel. Before jetting off to the Florida Keys, ask yourself why you want to take your cat along. To make you happier? Or to make your pet happier? If you cannot swear that your cat would gladly submit to round-trip air travel to be with you, then leave it home.

Cats can travel as carry-on luggage or excess baggage on commercial flights. As carry-on luggage, they ride in the cabin with their owners. Because most airlines allow only one in-cabin animal per flight, make reservations early.

In-cabin carriers must be small enough to fit under the passenger seat: roughly 17 inches (43 cm) long, 12 inches (30 cm) wide, and 8 inches (20 cm) high. Minikennels, which are available from most airlines and pet shops, should be made of heavy-molded plastic and should meet airline specifications.

If someone else's pet claims the cabin space, your cat is excess baggage, in which case you will need a bigger kennel—one large enough for your cat to stand up and turn around in. Again, if the journey is more than three or four hours long, tape a small litter pan containing a small amount of litter to the floor inside the carrier. Cover the rest of the carrier floor with a towel or disposable diaper. To make this or any trip less stressful, put a favorite blanket or toy in the carrier. Make sure the toy is something soft that you can secure to the inside of the kennel.

Pets shipped as excess baggage travel with the passengers' luggage in a part of the plane that is illuminated and maintained at the same pressurization and temperature as the passenger cabins. Because oxygen is limited in the hold, you will need to make reservations for this section, too. If possible, get a nonstop flight or find a direct flight so your cat does not have to be taken off one plane and put on another.

Airlines require that traveling pets arrive with health certificates issued by a veterinarian within the last 10 to 30 days. Many states require vaccinations, particularly rabies shots, as well. Whatever the regulations, your cat should have a preflight veterinary checkup. Some airlines suggest tranquilizing a cat before putting it on a plane. If your veterinarian agrees, fine.

Do not feed your cat within 12 hours of flight time, and make that meal a light one. A little chicken and rice are better than kibble or red meat. Do not give your cat too much water before the flight, either.

Leaving Your Cat at Home

Many people are wary about leaving their cats in a boarding kennel for fear they will be upset by the experience or will bring home fleas or something worse. A happy alternative is the pet sitter, who will feed, groom, medicate, and pet your cat, clean its litter pan, call the veterinarian in case of emergency, and, if necessary, tuck your cat into bed at night. Pet sitters also will bring in the mail and the newspaper, take out the trash, water the plants, and leave the television on overnight to create the impression that somebody other than Toby or Bowser is home. All this for a fee not much higher than the daily rate at a boarding kennel.

Most cats, especially older ones, will be happier if they can remain home while their owners are away. Though deprived of their owners' company, Scottish Folds will still enjoy their favorite place to sleep, their arsenal of toys, and their customary food. They will be surrounded by familiar household smells; and, most important, they will not be exposed to strange noises or smells that could upset them or to other animals with fleas or contagious diseases.

Look in the Yellow Pages or ask your veterinarian where to locate a pet sitter. Perhaps a technician at the vet's office would be willing to pet sit while you are away. You might even call a boarding kennel and ask if there is a pet sitter on staff.

Wherever you find one, be sure to interview the pet sitter in your home before you hand over the keys. Ask for and check references, and make sure the pet sitter is licensed, bonded, and insured. An interview gives you and your cat a chance to evaluate the pet sitter. What's more, the pet sitter will not be a total stranger the first time he or she arrives to feed your cat.

If there are no pet sitters in your area, choose a boarding kennel as if you were choosing a summer camp for the kids: pay a surprise, midweek visit to the kennel and ask for a tour of the premises. Don't be shy about asking questions: Is the facility licensed? Is there a veterinarian on call around the clock? Who is the vet and what is the vet's phone number? Ask if your veterinarian would recommend the kennel. Call the Better Business Bureau to ask if there are any complaints on file about the facility.

Grooming and Physical Care

How Often Should You Groom?

Grooming is the art of removing dead hair from cats so that they don't have to remove it themselves. Like virtue, grooming is its own reward. The more dead hair you collect from your Scottish Fold, the less you have to collect from the furniture, the rugs, or your clothing; and the less likely you are to encounter a foul, oozing hairball while you are walking to the kitchen barefoot in the middle of the night.

Shorthaired Folds do not occasion as much grooming as longhairs do. Shorthairs remain glistening on one or two groomings a week, and they require infrequent bathing—say, at the summer and the winter solstices—if they are not being shown. Longhaired Folds, even when they are not being shown, want three grooming sessions a week and should be bathed quarterly. Longhaired Folds during their show careers will need grooming every other day and bathing before each show.

A well-raised Fold kitten should not be a stranger to a comb or brush. For a kitten not comfortable being groomed, kindergarten should begin as soon as your pet is settled in its new surroundings. Groom your Scottish Fold five to ten minutes every second or third day until it is used to being handled.

If you do not have a grooming table, and most cat owners do not, a table or a counter in the kitchen or the bathroom will serve your purpose well. Avoid grooming your kitten on any surface, the kitchen table, for example, where it is not allowed to venture. If you remove your pet from the table one day then groom it there the next, you could sow confusion in its young mind.

Grooming Tools

Before you begin grooming, lay out the tools required for the task. You will need all of the following tools some of the time and some of the following tools all the time. Your selection will be driven by the nature of the grooming session:
- comb(s) or brush(es)
- cotton swabs
- face cloth
- nail clippers
- lukewarm water
- mineral oil
- paper cup or other receptacle for dead hair

Combs and Brushes

You need only two combs to keep a shorthaired Fold looking smart: a flea comb and a grooming comb with teeth about $5/8$ inch (1.6 cm) long and $1/16$ inch (.2 cm) apart. In some combs the tight, flea-catching teeth occupy half the comb's length while the all-purpose teeth occupy the other half. If you add a third comb to your arsenal, select one whose teeth are closer together than $1/16$ inch (.2 cm). No matter what comb you choose, the teeth should be rounded, not pointed, or else they might inflict pain on your cat.

An adequate all-purpose comb for grooming a longhaired Fold has teeth that are $7/8$ inch (2.2 cm) long and are divided into two equal sections. The teeth occupying one half of the comb are almost $3/16$ inch (.5 cm) apart. The teeth occupying the other half are a little more than $1/16$ of an inch (.2 cm) apart. A good second comb for longhairs has teeth about $5/8$ inch (1.6 cm) long and a little less than $1/16$ inch (.2 cm) apart. In addition, some people prefer combs with teeth of alternating length, $7/8$ inch (2.2 cm) and $3/4$ inch (1.9 cm), for grooming longhairs, and others recommend combs with $5/8$ inch-long (1.6 cm) teeth that rotate as they move through the cat's coat because the rotating motion helps to remove dead hair delicately.

Brushes are available in various materials and shapes with bristles made of animal hair, plastic, or stainless steel. The tips of the latter are often covered with tiny, plastic balls. Some brushes have natural bristles on one side and stainless-steel or synthetic bristles on the other. Many people do not like nylon- or plastic-bristle brushes as they damage the Scottish Fold's coat and generate static electricity, which makes grooming difficult. The same caveat regarding the teeth on a comb applies to the bristles on a brush: the tips of the bristles should not be so sharp as to inflict pain on your cat.

Clipping Your Cat's Claws

Begin each grooming session by checking your cat's claws. With the cat facing away from you, either standing on a table or sitting on your lap, lift one of the cat's legs so that the lower part of the leg rests in your upturned fingers. Holding the leg securely but unthreateningly between the heel of your thumb and the tips of your middle, ring, and little fingers, grasp the cat's foot between your thumb and forefinger. Press down on the top of its foot with your thumb, spreading the toes and ex-

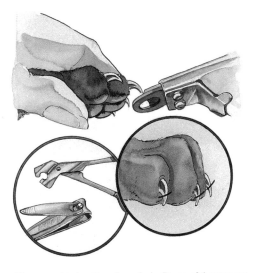

Claws need to be clipped regularly. Be careful not to cut into the quick—the visible, pink vein inside the nail.

tending the claws. Check each claw individually. If the end is blunt or rounded, leave it be. If the nail is honed to a talonlike point, clip it. Be careful to clip the hooked part of the claw only. Avoid cutting into the quick — the visible, pink vein inside the nail.

How to Comb or Brush a Cat

Because many cats are less amenable to being groomed in some areas (their bellies or hindquarters, perhaps) than they are in others, do not begin with one of these sensitive zones. Begin instead with an area such as the back of the neck or the base of the spine that usually invokes purrs.

The Comb-through Method

Comb or brush with the lie of the coat at first. Slide the comb into the coat at about a 45° angle. Do not push down constantly on the comb. Move it across the cat's body smoothly with your wrist locked. This technique also applies if you are using a brush, the only difference being that the bristles of a brush will meet the coat at a 90° angle.

With young kittens, and with some older cats, you will need to wield the comb or brush with one hand while you steady the kitten with the other. For example, place your free hand on the kitten's chest while you comb its back and sides; or place your free hand, palm up, on its underbelly while you comb your pet's hindquarters or neck.

To comb your cat's underbelly, lift its front legs with one hand and comb with the other. Place your free hand, palm up, just behind and above the midpoint of the cat's front legs. Lift its legs gently until the cat is standing on its hind legs with its back at about a 60-degree angle to the table. This technique is effective if you and the cat are facing the same direction. If the cat is facing you, place your free hand palm down instead of palm up.

Cats should be combed twice per grooming session, once to find flea dirt, skin rashes, or mats

The more dead hair you remove from your Scottish Fold with comb or brush, the less hair you will have to remove from your clothing, furniture, and rugs.

in the coat, particularly in the "armpits" of the cat's front legs. If you find flea dirt, a flea bath is in order. Skin rashes merit a visit to the veterinarian.

If you encounter a small mat about the size of a marble, do not try to rake it out with the comb or brush. Hold your cat against your body so that the mat is on the side of the cat farther from you. Take the mat in both hands, holding one half between the thumb and forefinger of your right hand and the other half between the thumb and forefinger of your left hand. Pull tenderly in opposite directions, being careful to pull parallel with your cat's skin. The mat should separate into two, smaller mats. Repeat the procedure, separating the two mats into four. The mats may then be small enough and loose enough to be tugged out carefully, one at a time, with the comb. If they are not, separate them once more and then comb them out.

Do not try to remove an overly large mat with the subdivide-and-conquer method just described. Make an appointment with a professional groomer or a veterinarian and have the mat shaved off.

Lift-and-Flip Technique

After you have completed your first comb-through, comb or brush your cat again. This time, instead of combing in long strokes, switch to a lift-and-flip technique to aerate the hairs and produce a soft, glowing look.

Starting at the base of the cat's tail, slide the comb or brush gently into the coat until you reach the skin. Then flick your wrist lightly in an upward, counterclockwise motion, lifting the hair against its natural lie. Continue this backcombing technique until you have reached the cat's head. Then run the comb or brush through the just-combed portion of the cat to return the coat to its natural lie. Repeat this process, which works on longhaired and shorthaired Folds, down the cat's sides, working from the spine to the rib ends.

To backcomb a shorthaired Fold's underbelly, lift its front legs as before, but make sure the cat is facing the same direction that you are. Instead of combing with the lie of the coat, begin combing just in front of the hind legs and work delicately toward the front legs. You need not use the lift-and-flip approach here. Use regular strokes instead, combing the hair toward the cat's front legs.

A longhaired Fold's underbelly can be back-combed front to back or back to front. The latter method requires that you face the cat when you lift its front legs. Begin combing right in front of your pet's hind legs. Instead of flicking your wrist counterclockwise (away from you) as you did when backcombing the cat's back and sides, flick your wrist clockwise (toward you). Repeat this stroke, moving the comb or brush an inch or so toward you each time until you reach the cat's front legs.

A Scottish Fold's legs are combed or brushed downward with short strokes. For a show-ring appearance, you can comb or brush the legs upward to give them a fuller look.

To groom the shorthaired Fold's tail, cup it on the underside with one hand about midway along the tail. Comb softly with the lie of the coat, moving the comb in 2- or 3-inch (5-7.6 cm) increments from the base to the tip of the tail. To comb the underside of the tail, lift the tail by its tip with one hand and comb with the lie of the coat from the tip toward the base of the tail.

Grooming and Physical Care

A longhaired Fold's armpits should be combed with care because many cats are sensitive in those areas. To get a leg up on this job, lift your cat's leg and comb gently downward until the hair has been separated. If your cat will tolerate the extra attention, comb once more, this time in the opposite direction.

To groom the longhaired Fold's tail, hold it gingerly by its tip. Move the comb or brush through the tail and toward you in short, incremental strokes, working from the tip to the base of the tail. Then comb the tail again, but this time use the lift-and-flip technique, flicking your wrist clockwise (toward you) as you work your way down the cat's tail from tip to base.

If your cat leaps off the table while you are grooming, fetch the cat and return it to the table, even if you were about finished. This lets your pet know that grooming is finished when you say so, not when it does.

Bathing Your Cat

The kitchen sink is the crucible of choice for most cat baths. A comfortable sink is at least 19 inches (48 cm) wide, 16 inches (41 cm) long, and 6.5 inches (17 cm) deep. Some sinks have built-in spray attachments. If yours does not, buy one at a hardware store, where you also can buy an adapter that will unite any spray attachment to any faucet.

To facilitate bathing, inveigle a spouse or a friend who has just dropped by for coffee to assist in the ceremony. One also is wise to have a cat carrier nearby with an absorbent towel covering the floor, in case your cat goes ballistic during the bath and needs to dry out before being released.

Before placing your cat into the sink, lay out the implements you will need for the ceremony:
- comb(s) or brush(es) or both
- two terrycloth washcloths
- regular or flea shampoo
- three bath towels
- cotton balls
- eight stacks of prefolded paper towels, about six panels thick
- blunt-tipped scissors
- toothbrush
- two small bowls of lukewarm water
- mineral oil in a squeeze bottle
- mechanic's-hand-soap solution (optional)
- dishwashing-detergent solution (optional)
- hair dryer (optional)

After assembling the requisite materials and your determination, cover the bottom of the sink with a rubber mat or a bath towel to provide secure footing for your cat. Turn on the water and adjust the temperature, testing with your wrist. If the water feels uncomfortably warm to you, chances are it will to your cat. Adjust accordingly. Make sure, too, that the house temperature is at least 72° (22° C).

If your sink has a single control lever for regulating temperature and water flow, turn the water off once you have adjusted the temperature. If your sink has separate controls for hot and cold water, leave the water running while you fetch the cat.

Before putting your cat into the sink, check its claws. If they need clipping, clip them. Some people also wrap a cat's feet and lower legs in masking tape to make sure the claws stay sheathed throughout the bath.

Now check your cat's ears. Remove visible dirt with a cotton swab or cotton ball moistened with hydrogen peroxide or mineral oil. Then put a small wad of cotton into each ear to prevent water from reaching the ear canal and possibly causing infection. Put a few drops of mineral oil into each of the cat's eyes to protect them from stray shampoo.

If your cat's face needs washing, clean it with lukewarm water and a face cloth. More-than-a-little-dirty faces can be cleaned with a weak solution of water and tearless shampoo. Squirt a few drops of shampoo into a bowl of lukewarm water, stir,

Grooming and Physical Care

and, using a washcloth, rub the solution carefully into the soiled areas on your cat's face. Rinse by dipping a clean washcloth into lukewarm water and rubbing the shampoo out of the fur.

When the moment of immersion is at hand, place your cat into the sink and let the good times and the water roll. If you are using flea shampoo on your cat, wet its neck thoroughly at once and lather it well to prevent fleas on the cat's body from hiding out on its face.

If your cat's tail is greasy, or if its coat is greasy in any area, take a handful of the mechanic's-hand-soap solution, rub it into the greasy spot, and work the solution into the coat. (To prepare the degreasing solution, combine half a can of hand soap, which is available at hardware stores, with an equal amount of water and let stand overnight.)

After massaging the hand-soap solution into the greasy area, rinse completely. You are finished rinsing when the water coming off the cat is as clear as the water going onto the cat.

Having degreased any offending spots on your cat, wet it down thoroughly with the spray attachment until your pet is soaked to the skin. Then apply the dishwashing-detergent solution, lathering the coat generously. Never lather past the cat's neck or you risk getting shampoo into its eyes. Put some shampoo on your toothbrush and brush the shampoo into the hair directly behind the cat's ears.

After your cat has been rinsed clean, apply regular shampoo, lathering copiously again. If you use a regular shampoo, rinse your cat after lathering. If you use a flea shampoo, check the label first to see if the manufacturer recommends leaving the shampoo on the coat for a while before rinsing. (A flea bath is only part of the frontal assault needed to rid your cat and your house of fleas. Consult your veterinarian or one of the summer issues of *Cats* or *Cat Fancy* magazines for advice about waging war on fleas.)

There are three secrets to a clean coat: rinse, rinse, and rinse. Some breeders use a premixed vinegar-and-water solution as a final rinse for optimum soap-scum removal. About half a cup of vinegar in a gallon of water is sufficient. Other people prefer a conditioning rinse manufactured for human use.

After your cat has been rinsed, take hold of its tail at the base with one hand, as if you were gripping a tennis racket, and squeeze gently, coaxing out as much water as you can. Repeat from midpoint to tip of tail and on each leg. Blot its legs, tail, and body with paper towels to absorb as much additional moisture as possible. Then remove the cat from the sink and wrap it in a towel, which can be warmed in the oven beforehand for your cat's postbath comfort.

Drying Your Cat

A shorthaired Fold in a warm house can be allowed to air dry after a bath. If you don't want a wet cat sitting on the furniture, confine your pet to the bathroom until the cat dries. Give it water and something to amuse itself with or to eat. The more special the food treat, the more likely your pet is to remember that baths end pleasantly. Your cat should be virtually dry in an hour.

Longhaired Folds can be allowed to air dry, too, but they end up looking like something the cat dragged in. Hair dryers are more efficient and produce better results. If you are going to use a hand-held dryer, put two or three drops of natural-tears solution or another moisturizing agent into your cat's eyes before you begin.

Cats do not take naturally to hair dryers any more than they take naturally to water. The best time to get your cat acclimated to the sound of a hair dryer is before you plan to use it. If you employ a hair dryer on your own hair, bring your cat into the bathroom or bedroom when you dry your hair. If you do not fancy the blow-dried look, run the hair dryer somewhere in the area where you feed your cat. Start the dryer on a low-speed setting before you begin preparing the cat's food. Leave the dryer running while the cat eats. If your pet shies at the sound, leave the dryer running and leave the room for a few minutes. If your cat refuses to eat, take up the food, turn off the dryer, and try again in a half hour. Eventually your pet will get hungry enough to eat with the dryer running.

Before applying the hair dryer, put a towel on the surface the cat will occupy while being dried. Wrist test the temperature of the air coming out of the dryer. The air should not be too hot or too forceful. The best dryers are the ones with separate speed and temperature controls and quiet-running motors.

Some people begin the drying process by placing their cats in carriers, the towel-lined ones that had been prepared for emergencies. If you try this approach, position the dryer so that warm air blows temperately into the carrier through the front door.

After 20 minutes or so, take the cat out of the carrier and place the cat on a table or counter. While directing a stream of warm air into its coat, comb cautiously. After the hairs in that area have been separated, move to another area of the cat. If you are attempting this job alone, be sure to use a hair dryer that has a stand into which you can set the dryer, thus leaving your dryer hand free for lifting the cat while you dry and comb its underbelly. Be sure that the dryer stand is resting on a towel or else as soon as you have the dryer adjusted to the proper angle for drying the cat's underbelly, the stand will start moving backward of its own accord.

When you have gone over the entire cat once with the dryer, begin again. This time concentrate on one section of coat at a time. Do not concentrate more than a minute or two on any one section because the heat from the dryer could become uncomfortable for your cat. To avoid this possibility, keep the dryer moving back and forth above the section you are working on.

As the coat becomes more dry, use the lift-and-flip technique (see page 34) to aerate the hairs and

For longhaired Scottish Folds, hair dryers are more efficient and produce better results.

get them completely dry. Use a toothbrush (or a flea comb) to groom the cat's face. If you notice that static electricity is raising cain with your cat's hair, rub an anti-static clothes-dryer sheet over its coat to smooth the hair into place.

If you are preparing your cat for a show, use blunt-tipped scissors to trim any stray hairs growing past the edges of its ears. Trim the ear furnishings, too, until they do not stand any higher than the ear does. Finally, trim any stray hairs extending over the cat's eyes.

Routine Ear Care

A Scottish Fold's ears are no more difficult to keep clean than are any other cat's ears. A few cotton swabs or cotton balls and some rubbing alcohol, mineral oil, or hydrogen peroxide in a small container are the only materials you need. Dip the cotton swabs or cotton balls into the alcohol, oil, or peroxide (the choices are yours) and swab the visible parts of the ear carefully. Do not plunge the cotton swab or cotton ball down into the ear canal any farther than the eye can see, or you might do some damage. If you wish to clean your cat's lower ear canal, buy a cleaning solution from your veterinarian and follow the instructions faithfully.

Nutrition and Diet

Proteins, Fats, and Carbohydrates

Because of their longstanding carnivorous habits, cats demonstrate several unique metabolic needs. The most celebrated is the need for protein (from the Greek *proteios*, meaning *primary*). Protein, which comprises more than 50 percent of an animal's dry weight, helps to build and to maintain cells. It provides energy through chemical breakdown, inspires muscle contractions, and, in the form of genes, sends hereditary instructions across generations. Digestive enzymes, insulin, the antibodies of the immune system, and most hormones are made of protein.

Protein is composed of units of roughly 20 amino acids, which themselves are composed of carbon, hydrogen, oxygen, nitrogen, and sometimes sulfur. Plants synthesize all the amino acids they need by combining nitrogen, carbon dioxide, and other chemicals. The cat, like most other organisms, can manufacture enough of only some amino acids. These are called dispensable amino acids, and they are made from other elements such as nitrogen and carbohydrate. The amino acids a cat cannot synthesize adequately are called essential amino acids. They must be obtained from protein in food.

Though cats prefer their food at room temperature, they are not the finicky eaters that advertisers claim.

If any of the ten essential amino acids is lacking in a cat's diet, food intake decreases, weight loss occurs, and (in kittens) optimal growth suffers. A few of the other effects of amino-acid deficiency include hyperactivity and spasms, development of bilateral cataracts, and neurological dysfunction.

Though growing cats require four times as much protein energy as do most other mammals, cats do not live by protein alone. Dietary fat, another essential nutrient, is a concentrated energy source, a carrier for fat-soluble vitamins, the wellspring of essential fatty acids, and a carnival for the cat's palate.

Cats fondly tolerate and readily use high levels of fat, but they cannot convert linoleic acid, an essential fatty acid, into the prostaglandin precursors linolenic acid and arachidonic acid. These substances, contained in animal products, must be present in a cat's diet. General symptoms of fatty-acid deficiency are dry coat, listlessness, poor growth, and increased susceptibility to infection.

The National Research Council (NRC) reports that as long as cats obtain sufficient fat and amino acids, they can exist without the sugars and starches contained in carbohydrates. Indeed, feline nutritionists observe that cats were originally domesticated because they would protect grain instead of eating it. Nevertheless, the cat-food industry learned more than 20 years ago that cats will eat carbohydrates if they are smuggled into the food dish inside processed corn wrapped in animal fat. This discovery led to the creation of dry cat food.

Vitamins and Minerals

Cats cannot reap the harvest from their food without the aid of vitamins, which combine with protein to create metabolically active enzymes that produce hundreds of important chemical reactions. Vitamins also assist in forming hormones, blood cells, nervous-system chemicals, and genetic material.

Nutrition and Diet

Four vitamins that cats require—vitamins A, D, E, and K—can be stored in the body's fat reserves. Other essential vitamins—the water-soluble B vitamins, thiamin, riboflavin, pyridoxine, niacin, pantothenic acid, and cobalamin—cannot be stored in the body.

Cats exhibit two unique vitamin requirements. The first is for preformed vitamin A, which they cannot manufacture by converting beta-carotene. The second is the need for niacin. This results from a cat's inability to synthesize niacin from tryptophan, an essential amino acid.

Although cats are mostly affected by the lack of vitamins, an excess of vitamins, especially A and D, also can be harmful. Vitamin A toxicity, the consequence of a liver-rich diet, causes skeletal lesions. Vitamin D toxicity, the upshot of unwarranted supplementation, results in calcification of the aorta, the carotid arteries, and the stomach wall.

If commercial cat food is labeled nutritionally complete, do not add vitamins or supplements to it, even when a cat is pregnant. Adding vitamins probably will upset the balance of vitamins already in the food and may cause vitamin toxicity. The only cats needing supplements are those not eating properly because of illness or those losing body fluids because of diarrhea or increased urination.

In addition to vitamins, cats need the following nine minerals: calcium, phosphorus, sodium, potassium, magnesium, iron, copper, zinc, and iodine. Because other species need them, cats also are thought to need manganese, sulfur, cobalt, selenium, molybdenum, fluorine, chromium, silicon, tin, nickel, and vanadium.

Minerals help to maintain tissue structure, fluid balance, and the body's acid-base (electrolyte) balance. If the acid-base balance is out of kilter too long, cats develop feline urologic syndrome (FUS). This syndrome, which includes a variety of disorders in the lower urinary tract, most commonly describes the formation of "kidney stones," urinary struvite crystals and calculi, that can cause potentially fatal urinary tract obstructions.

The NRC believes that inattention to the effects of diet on the acid-base balance may be a major factor in the incidence of FUS. The ingestion of abnormally large quantities of base-forming elements by the cat—an animal adapted to produce acid urine with a pH between 6.0 and 7.0—may be responsible for driving a cat's pH above the 7.1 level, where crystallization occurs spontaneously. Yet the council cautions against blaming an excess of any particular mineral, like magnesium, for causing FUS. The mineral composition of cat food must facilitate production of urine with a pH below 6.6. A litmus-paper test will demonstrate if a particular food meets this goal.

Because mineral requirements are interrelated, the same warning about vitamin supplements applies to mineral supplements.

Foods to Avoid

Table scraps: are not nutritionally balanced.

Raw meat: may contain parasites.

Raw fish: may contain parasites and may cause thiamine deficiency.

Raw egg whites: contain a protein that interacts with biotin, rendering it unavailable to the body. Biotin deficiency can cause dried secretions around the eyes, nose, and mouth and scaly skin.

Raw liver: contains an excess of vitamin A.

Bones: may lodge in a cat's throat or pierce the stomach or intestinal wall.

Dog food: does not contain enough protein.

Canned tuna for humans: causes vitamin E deficiency.

Chocolate: can diminish the flow of blood and cause heart attacks.

Liquids

Water is the most important nutrient needed to sustain normal cell function. Mammals can lose

Nutrition and Diet

nearly all their reserves of glycogen and fat, half their protein stores, and 40 percent of their body weight and still survive. The cat, composed of nearly 70 percent water, is in severe metabolic disarray if it loses 10 percent of its body water. Fortunately, cats can concentrate their urine and conserve water.

Water intake is primarily affected by diet. Because canned food is roughly 75 percent water, cats fed canned food will drink less than cats on a combination canned-dry diet or a dry diet exclusively. Whatever the case, give your cat fresh water in a freshly cleaned bowl every day.

As cats mature, they often become deficient in lactase, the enzyme that breaks down lactose in milk. Thus, many adult cats develop diarrhea from drinking milk.

Reading a Cat-Food Label

Cat-food manufacturers spend serious time and money trying to reinvent the mouse. This all-natural, 100-percent-nutritionally-complete-and-balanced meal in the soft gray pouch supplies the critical mixture of protein, vitamins, minerals, and essential fatty acids a cat requires.

Instead of mice on supermarket shelves, there are more than 90 brands of cat food in three genre: dry, semimoist, and canned. Dry food is less expensive and more convenient to use than canned and helps to reduce dental tartar to some extent. Canned food is more palatable, and because it is roughly three quarters moisture, is a better source of water than is other food. Cats on a canned-food diet are six or seven times less likely to develop feline urologic syndrome than cats on a dry-food regimen.

Semimoist food, because of its high chemical content, occupies a collapsing middle ground between dry food and canned. Semimoist comprises 5 percent by volume of all cat food sold in supermarkets. Canned food comprises 51 percent. Dry food makes up 44 percent.

No matter what its composition, food passes quickly through the cat's short gastrointestinal tract, which does not extract the nutrients as completely as a dog's plumbing does. The cat is best served, therefore, by highly digestible food.

All cat foods have one feature in common: their labels bristle with fine print. Precise editorial guidelines issued by the Association of American Feed Control Officials (AAFCO) govern the information on a cat-food label. The product name, the net contents of the package, and the species for which the food is intended must appear on the outside of the package. The manufacturer also must reveal the food's guaranteed analysis, expressed in minimum amounts of crude protein and fat and in maximum amounts of crude moisture and fiber. The name of the manufacturer, packer, or distributor of the food must appear on the package, but these parties need not disclose a street address if one appears in a current city or telephone directory.

Cat-food labels must enumerate, in descending order by weight, any ingredient for which AAFCO has established a name and definition. Ingredients not defined by AAFCO may be called by their common or usual names. The names of all ingredients must be equal in type size, and no ingredient may be listed under a brand or trade name.

If cat food contains artificial colors, they must have tested harmless to cats. Any additives in cat food must conform to federal requirements, be prior sanctioned, or be generally recognized as safe.

Cat foods must be identified as providing 100 percent complete nutrition for a particular stage (or for all stages) of a cat's life, or they must be labeled as intermittent or supplemental foods only. Many labels contain one of two statements: "Provides complete and balanced nutrition for the growth and maintenance of cats as substantiated through testing in accordance with AAFCO feeding protocols." Or, "This food meets or exceeds National Research Council recommendations for minimum amounts

Nutrition and Diet

of essential nutrients." Only snack foods and treats are exempt from this labeling requirement.

Foods labeled nutritionally complete and balanced for growth and maintenance, or for all stages of the cat's life, can be used from kittenhood through seniorhood, including motherhood. Foods "complete and balanced for maintenance of the adult cat" would not be satisfactory for a kitten or a pregnant or lactating queen.

If a food contains all the nutrients the National Research Council thinks it should, that is no guarantee that cats will benefit from those nutrients after consuming the food. Some nutrients may have been compromised in processing. For this reason, food whose nutritional performance has been established in feeding trials is preferred to food whose nutritional content is guaranteed to exceed NRC recommendations only at the pre-digestion stage.

Cat food labels understate the contents of the food they describe. If a manufacturer adds bone meal, which contains calcium and phosphorous, to a food, the label will say only "bone meal." Therefore, you won't find all the 40-plus nutrients that cats require listed on a package of food. The nutritionally complete-and-balanced statement is your clue that those ingredients are present in the food inside the package.

How Much and When to Feed

Kittens need relatively more food than adult cats require (see chart).

As the chart indicates, a ten-week-old kitten weighing 2.5 pounds (1.1 kg) would satisfy its daily food requirements by consuming 2.75 ounces (78 g) of dry food or 3.5 ounces (99 g) of semimoist food or 9 ounces (255 g) of canned food a day. A 10-pound (4.5 kg), inactive, adult cat would satisfy its daily food requirements by consuming 3.5 ounces (99 g) of dry food or 4 ounces (115 g) of semimoist food or 12 ounces (340 g) of canned

Daily Feeding Guidelines*

		Dry	Semimoist	Canned
		(ounces per pound of body weight)		
Kittens:	10 weeks	1.1 oz.	1.4 oz.	3.6 oz.
	20 weeks	.6	.7	1.8
	30 weeks	.45	.6	1.4
	40 weeks	.36	.4	1.2
Adults	Inactive	.32	.4	1.0
	Active	.36	.4	1.2
	Pregnant	.45	.6	1.4
	Lactating	1.00	1.3	3.3

*Adapted from *Nutrient Requirements of Cats*, National Research Council, 1986.

food a day. These amounts may be lower than those specified in the feeding instructions on the cat food package. As food labels underrepresent the contents of the package, they generally overstate the amount of food a cat needs.

Recommended feeding amounts are estimates based on data collected from many cat-feeding trials. A cat's metabolism, influenced by age and activity level, regulates food consumption. One 10-pound (4.5 kg) cat might need half a cup of dry food each day, whereas another might need two thirds of a cup. Pregnant and lactating cats will need more food than other cats.

Before deciding what to feed your new cat, find out what it has been eating. If its diet has been sound, continue with that product or products. Should you need to switch foods, which may happen if you buy a kitten raised on a homemade diet, mix new food with the old in a three-parts-old-to-one-part-new ratio. Every three or four days increase the new food while decreasing the old until the changeover is complete.

Though cats prefer their food at room temperature, they are not the "notoriously finicky" eaters that advertisers claim they are. Indeed, finicky eaters are made, not born. Two surefire ways to create a finicky cat are by feeding it the same food all the time or by feeding it people food. Give your cat a variety of foods and brands instead: meat and poultry for the most part, with fish for occasional variety. And lay off the people treats.

Overweight and Underweight Cats

Mature cats gain and lose in cycles that may last several months. A cat is overweight if its abdomen begins to droop; if you cannot feel its rib cage when you run your hands along its sides; if it sways from side to side when it walks; or if it develops bulges on either side of the point where its tail joins the body. You can prevent these symptoms from developing if you weigh your cat once a month and act accordingly. Whenever your Scottish Fold gains a pound, reduce its food by 20 percent. The easiest way is to feed your pet twice a day and to take up its food after 20 or 30 minutes. If you have several cats and you want to put one on a diet, you may have to feed that cat separately.

There is more than one way to thin a cat. Diet cat food, usually called *lite*, allows you to feed the same amount of food while lowering a cat's caloric intake. Lite food contains 20 to 33 percent fewer calories than does regular food. Lite and other special-diet foods should be fed only to those overweight, ill, or geriatric cats whose veterinarians recommend diet food.

A cat with constant access to food will eat as the spirit moves it, consuming several small meals a day rather than following a precise feeding pattern. Yet even though cats prefer round-the-clock noshing (feral cats, too, eat several small-prey meals each day), adults will adapt to being fed just once every 24 hours.

Adult Cats or Kittens

Because adult cats are so adaptable, feed at a time convenient for you. Some people feed "wet" food, either canned or homemade, twice a day. Others feed wet food once daily. Some feed wet food once a day and always leave dry food available for their cats. Some people, and many laboratories, feed dry food only.

Kittens are not as feeding-flexible as are adult cats. When kittens are being weaned, starting at three to four weeks of age, they should be fed three or four times a day. Reduce feedings to twice a day at six months, and, if you desire, to once a day after a cat's first birthday.

Cooking for Your Cat

For many people, feeding their cats is a sacramental experience involving zenlike preparation and adherence to detail. Most home cookers insist that their cats would not be as healthy, sparkling, stress resistant, and economical to feed on a commercial diet. They have the economical part right. Ground meat bought from a pet-food provisioner is much less expensive than anything that comes in a box, pouch, or can. But whether raw meat—sometimes cooked and always infused with vitamins, minerals, oils, and other molecular talismen—is better than commercial food is questionable.

Cats in the wild eat all of their prey, including the stomach content, and so they obtain a complete-and-balanced diet. Anyone feeding cats a diet based on raw meat must add the right vitamins and minerals in the right proportions. This is more complex than pouring calcium, a few tablespoons of vitamins, and some brewer's yeast into the meat and mixing thoroughly.

Unless you have some special intuition or knowledge that cat-food manufacturers with their million-dollar budgets and their battalions of feeding-trial cats have overlooked, leave the nutritional driving to the pet-food companies.

Health Care

The Healthy Cat

Like healthy kittens, healthy cats reflect their well-being in the way they look, behave, and tend to themselves. Healthy Scottish Folds have bright eyes and cool, slightly damp noses. Their gums are neither pale nor inflamed. Their ears are free of dirt and wax. Their bodies are fit and well muscled, not paunchy or obviously thin. Their coats are immaculately groomed, without bald patches, scabs, or flea dirt. The area below their tails is free of dried waste or discolored fur.

Though they spend prodigious amounts of time in sleep, as many as 14 to 18 hours a day, healthy Folds are otherwise active and alert. They display affection for their owners, concern for their appearance, and a keen interest in life and mealtimes. They are, in short, the cat's meow.

Cats possess voluntary and involuntary muscles. The latter, which are found in the alimentary canal, the urinary tract, and the respiratory system, are not controlled consciously by the cat. Voluntary muscles are secured to the skeleton by tendons. These "skeletal muscles," always arranged in pairs, work in cooperative opposition to each other.

Troublesome Indications

Perhaps the first suggestion that a cat is unwell is a lack of interest in food. One missed meal or a faint, desultory pass at the plate is not cause for apprehension, but the cat that misses two consecutive meals probably would benefit from a trip to a veterinarian—especially if its temperature is elevated or if it displays other symptoms of illness.

Indeed, some signs of illness are significant enough to warrant an immediate trip to the vet, as soon as you have called to describe the difficulty and to say that you are on your way over. The following list details some of those emergency symptoms. Do not consider the list exhaustive and do not try to use it as a diagnostic tool.

Take your Scottish Fold to the vet at once if your pet:
- has a deep wound or one that is still bleeding after pressure has been applied to it;
- seems drowsy after eating a foreign substance;

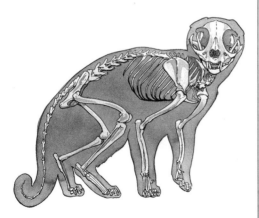

The skeleton. The 244 bones are classified into three groups according to shape: long, flat, and irregular. The radius and ulna in the front legs, the tibia and fibula in the hind legs are long bones. The scapula (shoulder blade) and the bones of the skull and face are flat bones. The metatarsals and metacarpals in the feet are irregular bones.

- stops breathing after chewing on a plant;
- has a temperature above 105°F (40.6°C);
- exhibits a sudden weakness in the hindquarters that makes it difficult to walk;
- has a red, ulcerated sore on its lips or any other part of its body
- develops an abscess that is warm and painful to the touch;
- has a runny nose accompanied by a temperature above 103.5°F (39.5°C), pale gums, or weakness;
- shows any evidence of trauma accompanied by shortness of breath, a temperature of 103.5°F (39.5°C) or more, pale gums, or lethargy;
- vomits and appears lethargic, attempts to urinate frequently, and has a temperature of 103.5°F (39.5°C) or more, and/or bloody stools;
- has diarrhea, bloody feces, an elevated temperature, or is vomiting;
- is constipated and strains at the stool while failing to defecate.

Call your vet for advice and an appointment if your cat:

- has abnormally thin stools and an elevated temperature;
- has a temperature between 103.5 and 105°F (39.5–40.6°C) and other signs of illness;
- begins drinking more water than usual and urinating excessively, has diarrhea, is lethargic, or has an elevated temperature;
- has a decreased appetite and is coughing, vomiting, or has diarrhea;
- exhibits general lameness in any leg for more than two days;
- develops a swelling that is warm and painful to the touch;
- has a runny nose accompanied by lethargy, pus in the eye, or rapid breathing;
- has a cough accompanied by an elevated temperature, difficult breathing, and lack of energy;
- has foul-smelling breath, is drinking water excessively, eating frequently, urinating frequently, yet appears lethargic;

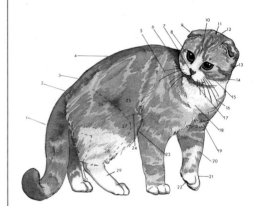

The external anatomy of the Scottish Fold cat.

1. tail	11. crown	21. metacarpus
2. base of tail	12. occiput	22. pad
3. rump	13. neck	23. elbow
4. back	14. nape	24. belly
5. withers	15. cheek	25. rib cage
6. shoulder	16. whiskers	26. upper thigh
7. nose	17. throat	27. knee joint
8. eye	18. chest	28. lower thigh
9. ear	19. upper arm	29. metatarsus
10. forehead	20. lower arm	30. hock

- has diarrhea accompanied by dehydration. (A cat is dehydrated if you take a pinch of skin from over its spine between your thumb and forefinger, lift the skin away from its body, and let go of the skin, which then does not spring back immediately into place.)

Top: Sherecon's Fold On A Minute, a silver classic tabby-and-white male, bred by Mandy Hemphill and owned by Hemphill, M. Gordon, and T. Warren, was the Cat Fanciers' Association's fifteenth best kitten for the 1989–1990 show season.
Bottom: A semilong coat, a flattering addition to the Scottish Fold, creates an altogether fetching appearance.

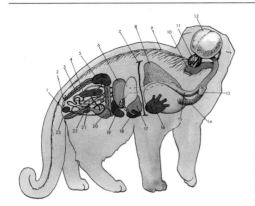

The internal organs.

1. testicles	9. spinal cord	18. gall bladder
2. anus	10. sinus cavities	19. spleen
3. large	11. mouth cavity	20. bladder
intestine	12. brain	21. small
4. pancreas	13. larynx	intestine
5. kidney	14. trachea	22. spermatic
6. stomach	15. esophagus	cord
7. diaphragm	16. heart	23. penis
8. lung	17. liver	

Preventive Health Care

A study published by the American Veterinary Medical Association (AVMA) in 1988 revealed that 60 percent of the cat owners in the United States had sought veterinary care for their animals during the preceding year. This represented a 26-percent increase over the number of owners who had taken their cats to a veterinarian in 1983. Unfortunately, the AVMA study also revealed that two out of every five cats in the United States received no medical attention, not even for an annual booster shot and physical examination.

Top left: A silver mackerel tabby-and-white.
Top right: A polished example of the dense, plush coat required on Scottish Folds.
Bottom: The three fold-eared kittens and the straight ear on the right display the "what-me-worry?" expression that characterizes their breed.

The AVMA data reminds us of the obligations incumbent upon all cat owners. These obligations include prompt, competent, and kindly medical care when necessary; a safe, clean, comfortable, indoor environment; a balanced, nutritious, invigorating diet; a yearly examination and booster shots; and habitual, loving human companionship.

Preventive health care begins with the annual trip to the veterinarian for a thorough physical examination and booster shots. In the basic examination, the veterinarian ruffles a cat's coat to check for softness, sheen, and texture, broken hairs, scales, fleas, flea dirt, and ringworm. The vet may also test for dehydration. In addition, the vet looks into the cat's eyes and ears, examines its teeth, listens to its heart and lungs, then palpates its kidneys and liver. Unless there is a reason why a cat should not receive them, the vet then administers the necessary booster shots.

Young, healthy Scottish Folds do not need as close or as costly an inspection as might older cats or cats with complex medical histories. Cats ten years old and more—or cats that have had medical problems in the past—may need additional tests to check for diabetes or to monitor blood chemistry, thyroid level, cholesterol, kidney and liver functions, and other conditions. The final component of a cat's annual checkup is the fecal examination. (See Internal Parasites, following.)

Vaccinations

During gestation, kittens normally inherit immunity against various diseases from their mothers. Thereafter, kittens are usually protected by antibodies in their mothers' milk until they are roughly eight weeks old. Because this passive or inherited immunity interferes with kittens' ability to produce antibodies, they generally are not vaccinated until they reach eight weeks.

The trick in vaccination science is to stimulate the body's immune defenses without causing disease. Thus, when a kitten is vaccinated, a small quantity of vaccine designed to protect against one or more feline afflictions is introduced into the kitten's bloodstream. Immunization, the desired end product of vaccination, is the process by which the immune system recognizes foreign proteins (or antigens) in a vaccine. Once the immune system recognizes these intruders, it manufactures protective proteins (or antibodies) and white blood cells that ingest and remove foreign material from the body.

That initial disease-fighting response, which is low grade and not entirely effective, begins about five to ten days after a kitten has been vaccinated. A second vaccination, which incites a more vigorous, lasting response, is given three to four weeks later.

Vaccines can be introduced into a kitten's body in one of three ways: intramuscularly, intranasally, or subcutaneously. The choice of vaccine and administration method are influenced by circumstance.

Killed vaccine: A veterinarian confident of obtaining effective immunity by using a killed vac-

cine, one that cannot cause disease or replicate itself, generally will do so because killed vaccines possess greater stability and offer maximum safety. A veterinarian who suspects that a kitten might be immunosuppressed also would use killed vaccine because it does not contain live virus.

Modified-live vaccines: These are chosen when a faster, more broad-based, immune-system response is desired. Because modified-live viruses continue to replicate in the kitten or cat, they confer a relatively long-term immunity.

Intramuscular or subcutaneous inoculation: A veterinarian using a killed or a modified-live vaccine can administer it intramuscularly or subcutaneously. The latter route generally prevails, not because of any physiologic advantage in invoking an immune-system response, but simply because it is more comfortable for the kitten. If, for some reason, greater speed of entry into the bloodstream is a factor, intramuscular injection is favored.

Intranasal inoculation: This is an important consideration when it is necessary to vaccinate against the upper respiratory viruses that enter the body through the nasal passages. Intranasal inoculations, which are limited to modified live vaccines, produce a local immune response on the linings of the nasal passages. This response, which can be important in blocking the early phase of infection at the source, may not be produced as readily from systemic vaccination paths.

Most kitten vaccinations are administered in a three-way injection designed to confer immunity against feline panleukopenia, feline viral rhinotracheitis, and feline calicivirus. Fewer than one percent of healthy kittens vaccinated in this manner at the proper age with the right dose of a properly stored vaccine will fail to produce an immune response. The same can be said of the rabies vaccine, but not the feline-leukemia-virus vaccine.

Like failure to develop immunity, severe allergic reactions to vaccination are rare. If they occur, the kitten should be taken back to the vet-

A major part of good health care is the annual trip to the veterinarian for a thorough physical examination and required vaccinations.

erinarian at once. It is a good idea, therefore, to schedule vaccinations for early in the day so that if you have to rush a kitten back to the vet, the office still will be open.

Next to the vaccine, the most important factor in developing immunization is the veterinarian, Anyone buying a kitten from breeders who give their own shots is foolish for not insisting that the kitten be examined by a veterinarian, preferably before the first vaccination is administered. For no matter how advanced the technology for producing vaccines might become, a vaccination is only as good as the exam that preceded it.

External Parasites

Parasites are living organisms that reside in or on other living organisms (called hosts), feeding on blood, lymph cells, or tissue. Parasites that dwell inside their hosts are called internal parasites (or endoparasites). Those that prowl on the surface of their hosts are called external parasites (or ectoparasites).

The cat's external parasites include fleas, ticks, flies, lice, larvae, and mites. In addition to damaging skin tissue, this motley collection of insects and arachnids may transmit harmful bacteria and menacing viruses to their hosts. In significant quantities, external parasites can leave their hosts devoid of energy, weaken their resistance to infection and disease, and infect them with a number of diseases or parasitic worms.

The presence of external parasites is usually revealed by skin lesions, hair loss, itching, redness, dandruff, scaling, growths of thickened skin, or an unpleasant odor. If any of these symptoms appears, take your cat to the veterinarian for a diagnosis. Cats infected with mites most likely will have to be isolated from other cats and treated with parasiticidal dips, powders, ointments, and shampoos.

Internal Parasites

There are four types of internal parasites that thrive in the cat: protozoa, nematodes, cestodes, and trematodes.

Protozoa: These one-celled organisms may contain specialized structures for feeding and locomotion. The protozoan most familiar to cat owners is *Toxoplasma gondii*. It can cause retinal lesions, calcified lesions in the brain, which are sometimes fatal, or water in the brain cavity of newborn infants whose mothers were infected by *Toxoplasma* during pregnancy. Children infected by *Toxoplasma* postnatally may develop a rash, flulike symptoms, heart disease, pneumonia, retinal lesions, and a fatal central-nervous-system infection.

To avoid *Toxoplasma* infection, pregnant women should not clean litter pans, or they should wear disposable rubber gloves if they do. Children, of course, should not be allowed to play near litter pans.

Nematodes: These somewhat resemble earthworms. The nematodes most often troubling to cats are roundworms and hookworms, whose presence can be detected through a stool-sample analysis.

Cestodes (or tapeworms): Not amenable to identification by stool-sample analysis, these worms, which are carried by fleas, are best identified by the ancient Egyptian technique of lifting a cat's tail and peering studiously at its anus. During this examination, the inspector is looking for small, white tapeworm segments that look like reborn stir-fried rice.

Trematodes: These tiny flukes live in the small intestines of their hosts. Because cats generally become infested with trematodes after eating raw fish, frogs, or small rodents—and because conscientious Scottish Fold owners do not allow their cats outdoors—there is little chance that readers of this text will need to worry about trematodes infecting their cats.

The life cycle of a tapeworm. The flea, which carries microscopic tapeworm larvae, bites a cat, transmitting the larvae to the cat. The larvae migrate to the intestine, where they develop into a mature tapeworm composed of many flat segments. Each segment absorbs nutrients from the contents of the intestine.

Worms, despite their repugnance, are not difficult to eliminate. If your cat needs to be dewormed, use a product prescribed by your veterinarian, and be sure to use it according to instructions.

Dental Problems

A cat's teeth should be white and clean, and its breath, while it lacks the freshness of peaches and cream, should not smell like freshly scattered fertilizer either. Cats have 30 adult teeth, which should have replaced and augmented the 26 deciduous or milk teeth by the time a cat is six or seven

months old. (Milk teeth begin to appear when a cat is about four weeks old.)

The gums and tissues of a cat's mouth should be pink, but for the black pigment spots that some cats have on their gums. Firm feeling, pink gums that adhere snugly to a cat's teeth are a sign of good health. Pale gums are a warning that a cat may be bleeding internally or suffering from anemia or any of a number of systemic diseases.

Gingivitis

Gingivitis, whose presence is advertised by a raw-looking, red line in the gums just above the teeth, is a frequent and a stubborn problem in cats. Mild gingivitis may be tolerated by a cat without causing any ill effects. More serious gingivitis is accompanied by drooling and bad breath.

Gingivitis can result from an accumulation of plaque and tartar on a cat's teeth. When plaque spreads beneath the gums, it inflames them, causing redness, swelling, and eventual loosening of the teeth. Gingivitis also can be caused by viruses

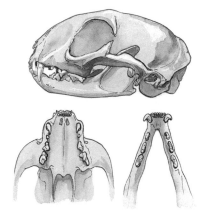

The cat's skull reveals the large eye sockets of an efficient night hunter. Though its jaw is short and it has fewer teeth, 30, than any other carnivore, the cat is well equipped to deliver a lethal bite and to tear off bits of food.

such as feline calicivirus and feline leukemia virus.

Those owners blessed with patience and with tolerant cats can clean their cats' teeth by rubbing them with a soft cloth (a cotton swab, a clean finger, a child's toothbrush, or a gauze pad) that has been dipped into dilute hydrogen peroxide, bicarbonate of soda, or saltwater. Do not use human toothpaste on your cat.

Whether your cat allows you to "brush" its teeth daily, weekly, or when the moon is new, its teeth should be cleaned professionally at least once a year.

Nursing a Sick Cat

The way a cat sees it, the best thing you can do for it when it is sick is to leave it alone. Cats appreciate and seek the regenerative power of solitude. They expect you to appreciate and respect that power as well. Thus, to nurse a sick cat is to strike a balance between respecting its desire for privacy and helping it to recover.

Not surprisingly, cats do not make the greatest patients. They resist taking pills as though they were being poisoned. They lick any "foreign" material from their coats, especially if it is medicated. They object to being force-fed, and because their instincts tell them they are vulnerable and, therefore, ought to hide when they are sick, they must often be caged in order to be accessible when it is time for 2 A.M. medication.

For these reasons, the seriously ill or injured cat is better left to the ministrations of your vet. Your cat will miss you while it is there, and you will miss your pet, but at least it will not associate you with pills and other unpleasantries.

Lesser ailments and convalescence should be weathered at home in familiar surroundings. This means, of course, that pills and medications must be administered by familiar hands. Namely, yours.

The first principle of home nursing care is that sick or convalescing cats should be isolated from other cats. The second rule is that persons handling sick or convalescing cats should wash their hands thoroughly and change their clothes before handling other cats. In fact, anyone handling a sick cat would do well to wear rubber gloves. What's more, all bedding, food dishes, water bowls, and litter pans used by any cat suffering from a contagious disease should be disinfected with a nontoxic antiseptic. All leftover food, litter, soiled dressings, excrement, and other waste should be sealed in a plastic bag and placed immediately into an outdoor trash can.

Sick cats are best confined to a double cage, 22 inches (56 cm) deep and tall and 44 inches (112 cm) wide, in a warm, quiet, draft-free room. The cage should contain a litter pan, food dish, water bowl, and a cozy cat bed for the patient. Towels around three sides and over the top of the cage also may make your patient feel more secure. Though a cat might not be up to playing with toys, a hanging toy spider in one corner of the cage eventually may prove diverting. If the patient must be kept warm, put a cardboard box, with one side cut down for ease of entry and exit, in one corner of the cage; and put a heating pad covered with a towel in the bottom of the box. Leave a radio, set to an easy-

Sick kittens or cats often will eat highly palatable food such as meat for babies from a spoon. Cats also will swallow pills that are smuggled into baby food.

listening or a nonradical talk station, playing softly. Groom the cat as usual if your pet will tolerate such. Otherwise, just hold and pet it gently. Do not spend too much time with it. Sleep is the second-best medicine in most cases.

Because many sick cats are not eager to eat, you will be challenged to concoct something that your cat will find palatable. Forget balanced diets for the moment. Feed a sick Fold anything it will eat. Because cats recovering from upper respiratory infections may not be able to smell most foods, use strong-smelling food like sardines or tuna fish or meat that has been seasoned liberally with garlic. If a cat accepts any of these, you can balance the menu as time passes.

Sliced turkey breast from the deli is a great favorite of sick cats. So is baby food. Some cats will eat a molasseslike, high-calorie food substitute available from your veterinarian.

To make sure that the patient does not become dehydrated, resort to any fluid you have to in order to get it to drink: water, beef broth, chicken broth, or evaporated milk mixed with baby cereal, egg yolk, karo syrup, and a pinch of salt. If your cat is extremely weak, you may have to give it fluids with an eye dropper or a syringe. (See Supplemental Feeding, page 75.)

Pilling

Pilling a cat is always a tenuous proposition at best. Some people seem to have been born with a knack for pilling. They grasp the top of a cat's head in one hand, pinching the corners of its mouth with thumb and middle finger or ring finger to force the mouth open, drop the pill onto the back of the cat's tongue, jab an index finger quickly against the back of its throat, withdraw the finger, hold the cat's mouth shut, then blow quickly into the cat's face to startle it and make it swallow.

Persons lacking this agility and self-confidence resort to pill guns, which still require that someone pry open a cat's mouth to insert the gun, or to hiding ground-up pills in butter, a lump of ham-

burger, or a mound of baby food. Whatever technique works, praise your cat for taking a pill and give it a treat afterwards.

Force-feeding

Force-feeding is less strenuous on your cat, and your pet's initial resistance may subside when it realizes that the stuff you are insinuating into its mouth tastes good. The technique for force-feeding is similar to that for pilling. Hold the cat's head from the top. Place your thumb against one corner of the cat's mouth and your middle finger or ring finger against the other corner. Squeeze the cat's mouth open. Put a dollop of food on the index finger of your free hand and rub it onto the roof of your cat's mouth. Relax the pressure on the sides of its face, allowing your cat's mouth to close, but keep its head restrained or else the cat might shake the food out. Putting a small dab of food on the cat's nose, from which it promptly will lick the morsel, is another way of getting your pet to take some nourishment.

If you are feeding liquid foods, put them into a syringe, open the cat's mouth as above, then squeeze some of the liquid into the pocket formed where the cat's upper and lower lips meet. Administer the liquid slowly, allowing the cat time to swallow. Five-cc syringes are easily manipulated. Buy a supply of them and change them frequently.

Skin Medicating

After applying any skin medication, hold your cat or play with it quietly for a few minutes to distract it so that your pet will not lick the medication off at once before it has had a chance to do any good. If skin medication must remain undisturbed for a longer period of time, ask your vet to show you how to fashion an Elizabethan collar that will prevent the cat from licking itself.

When the business of pilling, force-feeding, or medicating your cat is finished, apologize for the intrusion and explain that you really are trying to help. Then sit with your pet quietly for a while, commiserating.

Understanding Scottish Folds

The Cat in Perspective

No animal has had more unfortunate press than the cat. Deified during the Egyptian empire, vilified in the High Middle Ages, romanticized by everyone from Lewis Carroll to Ernest Hemingway, the cat remains grievously misunderstood for being so frequently misrepresented. Neither demon nor deity—and certainly not the haughty curmudgeon that some cartoonists and a few retrograde feature writers would have us believe—the cat deserves a more measured interpretation.

Though many feline myths warrant exposure, let the record show, at least, that cats as a race are not sly, enigmatic, arrogant, remote, ethereal, intimidating, or all that terribly complex. Nor were they created so that humans might caress the tiger. A cat is nobody's stand-in. And for all their quiet sovereignty—not to mention their seeming inclination to do what they wish while getting what they want—cats are quite willing to dance attendance on our comings and goings as if they were front-page news. The cats' dance, however, is a minuet, not a polka. Their song a chanson, not an anthem. Their poetry a lyric, not an epic. And while they are capable of playing the clown, they are quick to repair any pulls in their dignity.

"So perhaps a small part of the cat's notorious reserve and aloofness is something like whistling in the dark," observed prize-winning author Lloyd Alexander over three decades ago, long before cats had become ubiquitous fixtures on greeting cards and coffee mugs. "A cat's life can be as difficult as our own. And it may be that we comfort them for being cats as much as they comfort us for being human."

Domestication and Feline Behavior

The transcendent clue to understanding the cat is contained in the circumstances of its domestication. According to zoologist F. E. Zeuner, humans had domesticated at least a dozen animals before establishing a relationship with the cat roughly 3,600 years ago, a relationship that was initiated as much by the cat as it was by anyone else.

All animals domesticated before the cat—dogs, reindeer, yaks, and pigs among them—had lived in some kind of communal arrangement on which their biological and social well-being depended. Consequently, they all exhibited certain predictors of domestication: chief among them are membership in a large social group, acceptance of a hierarchical group structure, and a promiscuous lifestyle. But with the exception of promiscuity, the cat did not score high on these or most other variables that correlate with subsequent domestic status.

The ability to function in a tightly structured group contributes more than any other attribute to ease of domestication and to an animal's attachment to the domesticating species. This ability further explains, by its absence, why the cat does not regard humans with the same incessant affection as the dog or the same patient stoicism as the horse. These species follow the lead of the dominant member of the pack or herd, usually the alpha female. In an equine herd, for example, when the alpha mare stops to graze, the herd stops, too. When the mare takes off at a gallop, the herd follows. When the mare decides to rest, the herd settles down as well.

This centuries-old, follow-the-leader instinct disposes Trigger and Lassie to accept humans as the top dogs in their lives; but no such instinct prevails upon Garfield, who kept his own hours and his own counsel for thousands of centuries before signing a series of one-generation-only contracts to do light mouse work for humans. Therefore, whereas the dog is prewired to seek the goodwill of the alpha human, the cat is inclined to offer its friendship to such as deserve it.

What's more, the interval since the cat was first domesticated is but a blink in time's steady gaze. And as Zeuner has remarked, cats are "an instructive example of a species which is only in the first stage of domestication, perfectly capable of still becoming feral, and comparatively little altered" vis-á-vis its distant ancestors. Indeed, one could argue that pedigreed cats are the only truly domesticated felines because they are the only cats from whom we have usurped reproductive choices—an important element of the domestication process.

People have been arranging unions between pedigreed cats for no more than 120 years, and most of those unions were contrived on the basis of conformation not temperament. Nonetheless, there are already significant behavioral differences between domestic and pedigreed cats; and the latter, by and large, are more dependent on and more closely bonded to humans than are most domesticated and virtually all feral cats.

Perhaps in time the pedigreed cat will evolve into a companion more fawning than formal. Cats are known for their ability to exploit the most precarious of niches. If people want cats to fetch the newspaper—and set about breeding cats selectively with that end in mind—the late-twenty-first century feline no doubt will be described by writers as categorically different from the cat of the late-twentieth century. Who is to say, in fact, that the capacity for a more involved relationship with humans has not been part of the cat's repertoire all along—a talent the cat has been patiently waiting for us to discover?

Communal Living

In the back alleys of our cities, the backyards of suburbia, and the back woods and countryside of rural America, feral cats lead mostly first-person-singular lives. Low population densities, well-established rituals, clearly defined territories, limited and rather circumscribed interactions between adult cats, and one-tom-per-commonwealth living arrangements characterize the feral cat's existence.

Cats that live indoors, particularly in multicat confederations—in exchange for regular meals and climate-controlled lodging—are asked to abide conditions that violate the natural order. In one British study of cat-population densities, researchers found that feral cats in East London, where cats live in the most crowded conditions, had two-hundredths of an acre or 871 square feet (81 square m) to call their own. Yet few households and fewer catteries are large enough to provide this minimal acreage for every cat in residence. Obviously, indoor cats must live in smaller "territories" than do outdoor cats and, in multicat households, must tolerate greater interaction with other adult cats. These departures from a cat's natural life-style can lead to deviations in natural behavior and to greater susceptibility to stress and disease. The logistics of communal living may cause some cats to try to dominate others in the course of establishing a pecking order with regard to who eats before whom and who sleeps in what window. Crowded living quarters may cause some cats to ignore their litter pans periodically and may

Cat owners should try to recapitulate the cat's natural world by providing furniture that extends an opportunity to climb and offers a secluded area for privacy.

result in the rapid spread of parasites or illness if one member of the community becomes infected.

The privilege of keeping cats—and it is a privilege, not a right—is accompanied, therefore, by the responsibility of keeping them healthy and content. The cat breeder and the multicat owner as well must be creative enough to find ways of recapitulating the cat's natural world in an artificial indoor environment—providing toys that inspire hunting and chasing, cat "trees" that extend an opportunity to climb, secluded areas that furnish privacy, and windows that afford an opportunity to observe the world from which indoor cats are excluded. In addition, catnip for the occasional high, homegrown grasses for nibbling, and comfortable beds for sleeping all should be part of the indoor cat's environment.

How Scottish Folds Communicate

Communication includes the exchange of thoughts, feelings, needs, moods, information, trust, and desires. It involves listening as well as speaking. Where the cat is concerned, it entails listening not only with our ears but with our eyes and speaking not only with our voices but with our gestures, too.

The Scottish Fold and its primary component breeds, the British and the American shorthairs, are not talkative cats. Except for when they are in season, Folds save their voices for certain occasions: meowing forlornly if they have been shut accidentally into a closet, grousing sharply if you have pulled their fur too abruptly while grooming them, or sounding the alarm when they want you to get up and fix breakfast. Folds may also, for no apparent reason other than the spontaneous expression of their joy at being alive and in your company, pop into your lap with a jolly *chirrup*. (There are, of course, other vocalizations that cats use when speaking to one another or at birds on the far side of a window.)

No matter what the occasion, when your Fold speaks to you, there is a reason. Folds seldom talk to admire the sound of their own voices. You should, therefore, always respond when a Fold speaks. The cat stuck in the closet wants to hear how sorry you are for its misfortune and how you will never let this indignity happen again. The cat whose fur has been ruffled wants a similar apology. The cat waking you up for breakfast would like a cheery "good morning" and some food on its plate. The cat who is making a joyful noise would appreciate a soft "Hello," an attentive "What is it?" or a fond "You don't say?"

A cat's most endearing verbal communication is the silent meow, a phenomenon that is not peculiar to Scottish Folds but which is no less captivating for being universal. A silent meow is just that: a cat opens its mouth and mimes the word *meow*, but no sound emerges. Silent meows function as greetings, terms of endearment, all-purpose, unspecified complaints, and as the feline equivalents of baying at the moon.

Scottish Folds are more likely to communicate with their bodies than with their voices. From the tips of their noses to the ends of their tails, Folds are like electronic bulletin boards on which a continuous series of messages flows.

Cats can generate at least three of those messages with their tails. Carried erect at a 90° angle to the body, the tail broadcasts a message of good cheer and camaraderie. Carried at a less jaunty angle and puffed out in bristling display, the tail is a declaration of war. Twitching slowly from side to side, the tail signals annoyance. The faster the twitch, the greater the itch; and if twitch turns to lash, beware. Fireworks are about to ensue.

A cat uses its hindquarters to declare affection and trust. This form of communication—in which a cat brushes past the object of its affection and then positions its hindquarters in firsthand proximity to the object's face—may take the cat-owning novice by surprise, especially if cat and novice are enjoying a nap together. Indeed, most longtime cat

Understanding Scottish Folds

Tail messages. Top: Carried erect, the cat's tail broadcasts a message of good cheer. Center: Carried at a less jaunty angle and puffed out in bristling display, it is a declaration of war. Bottom: Twitching slowly from side to side, it signals annoyance.

owners would prefer that their cats said it with flowers instead.

A more conventional expression of fondness is the full-body flop, a maneuver in which a cat lands first on its side, then rolls onto its back, finally ending up in a semicircle. This fetching invitation to a belly rub usually is inspired by a cat's exuberance at being stroked along its spine or scratched at the base of its tail. Be cautious in accepting this invitation, however, because many cats are ticklish on their bellies. When you reach past their upturned paws to scratch their bellies, you are putting your arm at some risk. Should the cat take it into its head to grasp your arm between its front paws and to rabbit kick with its back paws, your arm could be in for a shredding. Do not panic and try to with-

draw your arm suddenly. That will make your situation more perilous because you will be pulling your tender skin against your cat's claws. Instead of moving your arm backwards toward you, move it forward and down through the cat's front legs. Because that is the direction in which your upside-down cat's claws are pointed, you will be disengaging your flesh from their grasp.

Right side up, the Fold taps out a variety of messages with its paws. A paw raised softly to a person's cheek or laid gently on the arm is a sign of attachment. A series of taps on the leg or arm is an attempt to bring the human to attention. A smart *whap* with the claws sheathed is a warning that you have violated a cat's sense of propriety. Such warnings often are issued while a cat that is being groomed is touched in a spot that is sensitive or ticklish. Some cats also will strike at the hand that pets them. This is a curious, disconcerting, and somewhat puzzling response. Feral cats that react in this fashion to being petted can be excused on the grounds that they are not used to such affection or have not developed enough trust in people, but one is hard put to imagine why some domesticated cats react this way occasionally, too. Perhaps in the cat's mind there can be too much of a good thing.

Like its tail, a Scottish Fold's ears convey different messages and emotions. The ears' folded condition does not inhibit their mobility. Folds will swivel their ears in response to new sounds in the vicinity. They will flatten their ears and extend them to the side in response to a frightening stimulus. And they will curl their ears backward in anger.

Cats greet their two-legged and four-legged friends in well-defined ceremonies. A cat, its tail erect in greeting, will approach a friend and then rub its cheek against the cheek, neck, or face of that friend. This rite not only indicates cordiality, it is a request for permission to enter another individual's air space, and it leaves a trace of the approaching cat's scent on its friend.

Communicating with Your Scottish Fold

If cats had a book on our modes of communication, it probably would reveal that they are more comfortable when we are communicating with them on their level than when we approach them from a superior position. Cats are apt to associate creatures that loom large with predators. Therefore, when you are greeting a cat, especially a new cat or kitten, crouch down before you do and extend your slightly curled hand, knuckles facing away from you, toward the cat, allowing it a chance to sniff and rub up against your hand if the cat wishes. If the cat turns away from your hand, do not attempt to pet it right then because its behavior indicates a lack of interest in either you or your salutation.

In all your interactions with your cat, try to mimic its sense of order, civility, and decorum. Do not make any abrupt movements or any sudden, loud noises. Do not lift the cat up if it does not enjoy being carried, and by all means do not stare long and lovingly into its eyes. Cats regard staring as an insult.

Aside from communicating your joy in its presence, which you should do with hugs, pets, and kisses as well as words, the other message you will want to convey to your cat is your displeasure at something it has just done or is about to do.

The best way to teach your cat to refrain from doing something you do not want it doing is to establish an association between the proscribed conduct and an unpleasant occurrence. Suppose you are sitting at the kitchen table and your kitten races across the floor and begins climbing your leg, which kittens are wont to do. If its claws sink deep enough into your leg, you might scream in pain, and this might be enough to send your kitten on its way—for now. But even if the pain is not severe this time, reach down quickly, remove the kitten from your leg, set it on the floor facing away from you, and bark *No!* If your kitten assaults your leg again—even if not until the following day—remove it, bark *No!,* and clap your hands sharply for emphasis. Better yet, if you notice your pet eyeing your leg with bad intent, say *No!* before it gets a chance to leap.

The youngest feline capable of scaling a human leg eventually will connect your sharp voice and other unpleasant noises with its recent behavior. But even the wisest cat has a limited retention span, about 20 seconds to be precise. Thus, you are wasting your time and your cat's goodwill by taking it to the scene of a crime—a broken knickknack or a soiled spot on the carpet—and reprimanding it sharply for something that happened hours or minutes ago. The only lesson your cat will learn by this delayed reprimand is that humans sometimes act peculiarly for no good reason.

Greeting a cat whose acquaintance you have not previously made.

Cat Shows

Finding the Shows

Before entering a Scottish Fold in a show, first-time exhibitors should visit a few shows to observe prevailing customs and to appraise the competition. Cat magazines advertise hundreds of shows held each year in the United States and Canada. If these magazines are not available at the newsstand, call one of their subscription departments (see page 83) and ask to buy the latest issue. The association in which a cat has been registered (see page 83) also can provide information about shows it licenses. Newspapers often contain notices for local shows in the "Pets" section of the classified ads or in the notices of coming events in the "Living," "Life-style," or "Weekend" sections.

The Entry Form and the Show Flyer

A show advertisement provides the name, address, and phone number of the entry clerk for that event. Write or phone the entry clerk to request a show flyer and an entry form.

The flyer publishes the show hall location, the time the show begins, and the hours when exhibitors can check in. The flyer also discloses whether the show committee will provide litter, litter pans, and cat food for all entries, and what special trophies or prizes will be awarded at the show. Flyers announce the entry fee, the date on which the club will stop taking entries, and the judges who will officiate at the show. Flyers remind exhibitors that all household pet entries must be neutered or spayed, that all cats' inoculations should be up to date, that cats from catteries where infectious illness has occurred during the last 21 days are not allowed in the show hall, and (if local law requires) that exhibitors must bring along proof that their cats have been vaccinated against rabies.

On the entry form, an exhibitor provides the name of the cat being shown, its owner's name, the cat's breed, color, registration number, date of birth, parents, sex, and eye color, the class the cat will compete in, the name of the person, if any, who will exhibit the cat for its owner, and the name of the person, if any, with whom an exhibitor would like to be benched. (Each cat entered in a show is "benched" or assigned to a cage where it remains when it is not being judged.) If an exhibitor has any questions about completing an entry form, entry clerks will answer them cheerfully before nine or ten o'clock at night.

Once an entry form is completed, the exhibitor mails it with the appropriate fee to the entry clerk. Two-day shows cost $30 to $60, depending on the number of times a cat will be judged. One-day shows are proportionately less expensive.

The number of entries at a show usually is limited, and shows often reach their quota before the advertised closing date. To avoid being shut out, exhibitors should mail their entry forms at least two or three weeks prior to that date. If you enter a show and do not receive confirmation within two weeks after mailing your entry, phone the entry clerk to ask if the entry has been received.

The entry confirmation contains a facsimile of the cat's listing in the show catalog, directions to the show hall, a list of motels near the hall, and other information. Exhibitors should proofread the confirmation to be sure all names are spelled correctly, the cat's registration number is accurate, and the cat has been entered in the correct class. Errors should be reported immediately to the entry clerk. After checking the confirmation, exhibitors should keep it in a safe, easy-to-recall place.

Provisions for a Show

Cats at a show remain in their assigned benching cages when not being judged. Exhibitors are expected to bring curtains for the sides and back of the benching cage and a rug or a towel for the cage floor. Most single show cages are small: 22 inches (56 cm) long, wide, and tall. For an extra $10 to $20, exhibitors can order a double cage when they send in their entry blanks. A double cage provides more room in which a cat can stretch its legs, and the extra chair that comes with a double cage provides a convenient footrest for an exhibitor. Most double cages are 22 inches (56 cm) deep and tall and 44 inches (112 cm) wide.

Cage decorations vary with an exhibitor's taste, budget, sewing ability, and sense of style. Some exhibitors equip their cages with lavish, hand-sewn curtains and four-poster beds. Other exhibitors fancy a military-barracks look with bath towels held in place by metal clamps. A few exhibitors bring their own cages, which often resemble a cross between a habitrail for cats and a miniature intensive-care unit. Personal aesthetics notwithstanding, minimum show requirements decree that cage curtains be fastened securely inside the cage and that they cover both the sides and the back of the cage. Many exhibitors also cover the tops of their cages, creating a more cozy environment for their cats.

Like fashions in cage curtains, the number of incidental items packed for a show is determined by personal comfort. Some exhibitors trundle into a show hall with enough provisions for a two-month stay in a biosphere. Others pack more conservatively.

Nonammonia-based disinfectant is necessary for wiping down the benching cage and any suspicious surfaces in the hotel room. Pipe cleaners are handy for securing any loose corners of the cage. A small, TV-dinner-sized table is useful for grooming. A bath towel makes a good cover for the table. A cardboard litter pan takes the worry out of being far from home. Show committees always provide litter, and they usually provide litter pans; but the seasoned exhibitor always carries a small, disposable, cardboard litter pan just in case.

Cats should be transported to shows in sturdy, heavy-molded-plastic carriers. These are available

Basic Show Supplies	
regular comb(s)	flea comb
cotton swabs	cotton balls
paper towels	facial tissues
washcloth(s)	bath towel(s)
scissors	eye drops
cage curtains	cage rug
spray disinfectant	pen
pipe cleaners	can opener
bottle opener	cat toys
masking tape	adhesive tape
cellophane tape	first-aid kit
cattery cards	cat food
water bowl	litter scoop
small metal clamps	safety pins
cardboard litter pan(s)	spoon
entry confirmation	cat shampoo

brushes and grooming powder if applicable; a small, TV-dinner-sized table; magazine, book, or small TV; biodegradable paper plates; snacks and hors doeuvres; bottled water from home; small plastic baggies

at pet-supply dealers, pet shops, some airline cargo offices, and cat shows. The cat's journey will be more comfortable, especially if the ride is long or the cat is young, if the owner tapes a small litter pan to the floor inside the carrier. Disposable cardboard litter pans, cut in half (with the cut parallel to the shorter sides) and pleated back together, fit easily into a carrier. The rest of the carrier floor should be covered with a towel or disposable diaper.

Many exhibitors cover the outside of their carriers with fitted, quilted bonnets in cold weather. These bonnets, which resemble toaster covers, are available at shows or from companies that advertise in cat magazines. Exhibitors also can sew their own (if they are sew inclined).

Cat carriers. From bottom to top: an under-the-seat airline carrier; a standard carrier; a cage.

Show Hall Decorum

New exhibitors should arrive at the show hall early for check in. After obtaining their cats' cage numbers and a show catalog, the first orders of business are setting up the benching cage and finding out where the litter and the litter pans are stored. Many exhibitors spray the cage and cage floor (or bottom) with disinfectant and wipe it off carefully before decorating the cage and placing their cats in it. Cages are light enough to lift off their bottoms, which are supported by trestles about 3 feet (.9 m) high.

While the cage is on the floor, exhibitors easily can fit a rug or towel over the cage bottom. After placing the cage back on its trestle-supported bottom, lift up the top of the cage and install the cage curtains on the inside of the cage. Fill a litter pan with an inch (2.5 cm) of litter and place the pan at one end of the cage. Make sure the cage top is

fastened securely in case something in this foreign environment frightens your cat. Finally, put your cat into the cage with a favorite toy or two.

Because all show cages are double cages with a hinged, moveable divider in the center, exhibitors who get a single cage will be sharing a duplex with someone else. If that person already has set up a cage, be careful when spraying and decorating your half of the cage not to disturb your neighbor's cage or cat.

Some exhibitors feed their cats after the cats have finished sniffing about their cages. Other exhibitors, who fed their cats before leaving for the show hall, wait until later in the day to feed. In either case, cats should be offered water when they are settled in their cages. Some exhibitors leave a water bowl in the cage all day. Others offer their cats a drink periodically throughout the day.

If cats do not eat or drink in the show hall, exhibitors should offer their cats food and water as soon as they get home or to the hotel room.

How Cats Are Judged

A cat show actually comprises a number of individual shows held separately but concurrently in several judging rings throughout the show hall. With few exceptions, every cat in the hall is eligible to compete in every individual show. Each show is presided over by a different judge who presents awards independent of the decisions of other judges. Therefore, a cat chosen best in show by the judge in Ring 1 may not receive the same award —or any award at all—from the judge in Ring 2.

Individual shows and their judges are classified as either allbreed or specialty. In an allbreed show, all cats entered compete for awards. In a specialty show, only those cats of similar coat length, or conformation and type, depending on the association, compete against each other.

Whether an individual show is allbreed, longhair specialty, or shorthair specialty, competition is

Cat Shows

held in five categories: championship, altered, kitten, new breed or color (sometimes called provisional), and household pet. Championship competition is for unaltered, pedigreed cats at least eight months old. Altered competition is for neutered or spayed pedigreed cats at least eight months of age. Kitten competition is for pedigreed youngsters between the ages of four and eight months. New breed or color competition is for those breeds or colors that have not gained championship status. Household pet competition includes all mixed-breed, nonpedigreed cats, at least in theory. Many people today show pet-quality pedigreed cats as household pets. Whatever their particulars, household pets older than eight months must be altered before they can be shown.

The judging schedule is printed in the show catalog or on a separate sheet provided with the catalog. Exhibitors should circle the rings in which their cats are scheduled to be judged. Exhibitors also should check to make sure their cats' names and attendant biographical data are printed correctly in the catalog. If there are any mistakes in this information, the exhibitor should tell the master clerk immediately.

Cats are called to the judging rings via the public address system. When the first Scottish Fold numbers are called, begin listening carefully for your cat's number.

Be sure to have a secure grip on your cat while carrying it to the judging ring. Hold your forearm slightly extended, palm up, parallel to the ground. Position your cat so that it straddles your forearm. Cup the cat's chest in your palm, securing one front leg between your thumb and forefinger, and the other front leg between your ring and little fingers. Should your cat become startled, stop for a moment, bring your forearm close to your body, and use your free hand to comfort your cat.

Upon arriving at the judging ring, find the cage with your cat's number on top and place your cat into that cage. Fasten the cage door securely, then take a seat in the gallery.

At roughly 500 shows a year sponsored by six different North American associations, cats are judged on conformation and presentation.

Like most eagerly awaited events in life, a cat's interval on the judging table is brief and somewhat anticlimactic, about 90 seconds on the average. During that time, judges compare a cat to the standard for its breed (see page 17). After handling all the entries in a class or division, judges hang ribbons whose text and colors proclaim the placement of each contestant in the group that has merited a ribbon. Then the clerk will dismiss the class by saying, "These cats can go back," or simply by turning down the numbers on the tops of cats' cages.

After a judge has examined all the cats competing in a category—all kittens, for example—it is time for finals, the encore in which the judge presents the top ten contestants in that category. During finals, the judge introduces the cats, usually in ascending order of merit, until the best cat (or kitten or alter, as the case may be) has been held aloft in triumph.

Adult cats compete for titles that vary somewhat in nomenclature and requirements from one

Cat Shows

association to the next. New exhibitors can learn the requirements of those associations in which they plan to have their cats compete by obtaining a copy of the association's show rules (see page 83) or by talking to a veteran exhibitor.

All associations offer champion and grand champion titles, and most award other titles beyond those. Champion, the lowest-ranking title, can be won in most associations even if a cat is the only entry in its class. Titles beyond champion are earned by defeating specified numbers of other cats, including other champions, in competition.

Mark Twain, who knew something about human nature and cats, once observed that it is difference of opinion that makes horse races. The same applies to cat shows. Judges spend one to two minutes evaluating each cat. They often make more than two hundred of these rapid-fire assessments per show. For this expertise judges receive from 35 cents to a dollar for every cat they judge. (Exhibitors who disagree with judges' decisions sometimes complain that a judge's opinion is not even worth that.)

Whatever the outcome, exhibitors would do well to remember that when they enter a cat in a show, they are paying to learn what several judges of varying degrees of competence and experience think about the exhibitors' cats at a brief moment in time. Those exhibitors who keep this in mind and who remember that win or lose their cats still need to be fed tomorrow, will find that a cat show is a diverting way to spend a weekend.

Top: This glorious brown patched tabby-and-white female, bred and owned by Jean L. Grimm, was the Cat Fanciers' Association's twentieth best cat for the 1990–1991 show season.
Bottom left: The ears on this brown mackerel tabby blend seamlessly into the well-rounded contour of its head.
Bottom right: If you like an extreme head, you should love this big-eyed, short-nosed, brown classic tabby-and-white male, bred and owned by Lynn, Dyan, and Annie Odne.

Sexual Behavior of Cats

The Female's Heat Cycle

A heat cycle or season, more properly called estrus, is a period of sexual receptivity that occurs in most mammalian females, cats included. In the majority of female cats, estrus (from the Greek word for "mad passion") first occurs between 7 and 12 months of age. Male cats, which are said to be always in season, generally become sexually mature between 9 and 12 months of age.

Estrus in most female cats is prompted by an increase in available light. Thus, after being sexually inactive throughout the fall, cats begin to come into season in observation of the new year as the days begin lengthening gradually. Cats that are not bred during estrus normally go out of season after six to nine days.

The interludes between periods of estrus are called metestrus. They last as few as 3 or as many as 30 days, but the average length is 9 to 13 days.

Female cats repeat this in-a-while-out-a-while roundelay until March when, for reasons not yet known, many females stop cycling temporarily. By June, most unbred females resume cycling. They continue to do so until mid-September. If they are not with kittens by then, they remain out of season for about three months. This extended fallow period, called anestrus, may vary among breeds. In one study reported in the *Journal of Small Animal Practice* in 1977, 90 percent of the longhaired cats observed went into seasonal anestrus, but only 40 percent of the shorthaired cats did.

Top left: The gene for white spotting has expressed itself boldly in this brown classic tabby-and-white.
Top right: This black-and-white Fold looks as if it is dressed in formal attire.
Bottom left: This Fold's soft expression and delicate coloring are complemented by a retro-Victorian setting.
Bottom right: If Easter baskets contained cats instead of eggs, this white would make a perfect centerpiece.

Though the calendar says it is winter, the days have begun to lengthen gradually already. Female cats respond to this increase in available light by going into season.

Behavioral Changes During the Heat Cycle

As the days begin to lengthen in grudging increments following the winter solstice, the female cat's eye eventually responds to this increase in light by sending neurochemical messages to the brain, via the pineal gland. As a result, production of the estrus-inhibiting hormones prolactin and melatonin is curtailed, and the female soon begins cycling.

No one has reckoned with any precision the interval between the time a cat responds to a change in light and the time she goes into season, but there is usually no mistaking seasonal behavior. Females begin "acting funny" with the arrival of proestrus, a one- or two-day, minor squall before the storm. Females in proestrus act as though they sense a change in the weather. They become restless and vocal. They flirt with presumed suitors of either sex. They tread sporadically with their hind feet. They often become cloyingly affectionate to-

Females signal their willingness to mate by assuming the lordosis position: front end down, back end up, tail inclined to the side.

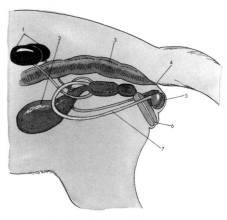

The male urogenital system.
1. kidney   5. testicles
2. bladder   6. penis
3. large intestine 7. vas deferens
4. anus

ward humans and sofa corners. Some females may allow males to mount them during proestrus, but penetration generally is reserved for subsequent dates.

After a day or two, proestrus gives way to full-tilt estrus, and the female is ready for an adult relationship. She will accept mating without much small talk, and she advertises her tractability by howling frequently day and night and by slinking about in the lordosis posture: low in the front, high in the rear, tail swept carelessly to the side. She is also wont to scurry out of doors if she is not properly chaperoned at this stage, returning a few days later—if she and her owner are fortunate—looking like something the cat dragged in and incubating a litter of mixed-breed kittens.

Managing the Breeding Process

Only healthy, well-adjusted females that have been in season at least once, are beyond ten months of age, and whose forebears have a history of trouble-free deliveries should be considered for breeding. And only those females whose pedigrees and, in most cases, whose show records suggest that they have a contribution to make to their breeds should be considered seriously.

Healthy, well-managed cats chosen for their reproductive potential seldom occasion medical or surgical emergencies. Unfortunately, some breeders work with animals that nature rightly would advise to remain childless, and in some minor breeds the available gene pool is scarcely big enough to accommodate selective breeding. Thus, subfertility and infertility are more common in the cattery than they are in the laboratory or in the field behind the house.

Because the Scottish Fold was assembled from several breeds and can be outcrossed to British and American shorthairs, it should be a robust cat, reproductively. Nonetheless, all breeders need to be prepared for most eventualities.

Unlike dogs, female cats display little if any vulvar swelling or vaginal discharge during estrus. Cat breeders must observe behavioral clues that advertise the time to breed their females. Or-

Sexual Behavior of Cats

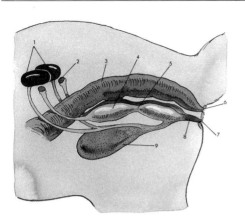

The female urogenital system.

1. kidney
2. ovaries
3. large intestine
4. uterus
5. cervix
6. anus
7. vulva
8. vagina
9. bladder

dinarily these clues are published in large, clear print, and there is no mistaking their meaning. But some females write in a cramped, illegible hand.

Indeed, some females have silent seasons. They do not call, tread, or otherwise suggest their availability. There is one straight-ahead solution to solving the riddle of the silent heat: allow the reticent bride to live with her betrothed until their union is consummated. This solution, however, is available only to those breeders who own their own males. The novice, who is best advised not to buy a male at first, must solve the riddle in other fashions.

There are fairly precise, scientific ways of determining when a cat is in season, but such technologies are beyond the ordinary measures a breeder needs to take to get a female bred. Novice breeders with silent-heat females typically solve this problem by finding a reputable, patient, and experienced breeder—with a savvy, seductive, and quality-producing male—who will take a shy

female in for stud service knowing that she may be staying more than a few days.

Once a cat is in season, breeders generally are able to introduce her to a male cat with no adverse consequences beyond ritualistic hissing and name calling. But mating, for some females, is more than a one-act play. Their scripts demand dramatic buildup, occupying several preliminary acts, before the denouement is reached. Some females, in fact, cavort like strumpets on their own turf but go out of season immediately when they meet their intended mates.

Coy, retiring, or even aggressive females often can be conditioned to accept a male's advances if they are exposed to an experienced, rational male before they come into season. Some breeders cage a female in the male's quarters while the male is permitted to greet her through the bars of her cage. (See Introducing Other Pets, page 29). Perhaps she could be placed in a large pen next to a male's or be allowed to run loose in the room where his pen is located. This conditioning should begin before a breeder expects the couple to get personal. How long before will depend on how shy or how lethal the female is in the male's company, but a week to ten days prior to opening night is a reasonable time to begin dress rehearsals.

When a female accepts a male's attentions, the pair should be left to themselves for three days whenever possible. Unlike the rabbit, who will ovulate faithfully at first breeding, the cat responds to mating stimuli, both single and multiple, in a random, nerve-wracking fashion; and researchers have yet to decide whether one mating is sufficient to effect ovulation in all cats. It may be for some females, but it is probably not sufficient for most. What's more, cats who ovulate in response to a single amorous encounter this season, may not be so accommodating the next.

Researchers further suspect that quality (the vigor of copulatory motion) and quantity (the number of copulations per estrus) govern the dispatch of the message sent from the cervix to the hypothalamus, telling it to release additional quantities of luteinizing hormone (LH), which conspires with the elevated level of estrogen in the cat's bloodstream to prompt ovulation. Cats that do not ovulate after one mating were, perhaps, not sufficiently stimulated, and hence the hypothalamus was never told that it was time to release additional hormone. Or perhaps the hypothalamus did release LH, but its level in the bloodstream did not remain elevated long enough to insure ovulation.

In a study conducted in the late 1970s, seven groups of 12 females were mated on different days of estrus and for varying numbers of times on those days. In the group allowed to mate once on the first day of estrus, only 1 out of 12 females ovulated. In the group allowed to mate once on the second day of estrus, 2 out of 12 females ovulated. In the group allowed to mate once on the third day of estrus, 3 out of 12 females ovulated. In the group that mated once on the fourth day of estrus, 4 out of 12 females ovulated. By contrast, in three other groups that were permitted to mate three times a day on either the first, second, or third day of estrus, 10 out of 12 females ovulated.

This study illustrates the importance of copulatory frequency on ovulation. Hence the suggestion that males and females be allowed to breed ad libitum, if possible, for at least three days.

Healthy males can copulate three times a day over a four- to five-day interval without a noticeable decrease in sperm concentration. If a male is being used frequently in a cattery and sexual exhaustion is a concern (or if a male becomes aggressive with his partners when not breeding), a mating regimen in which cats are allowed to breed three times a day at three- or four-hour intervals during the first three days of estrus has produced conception rates between 90 and 100 percent in several studies. This timetable insures that functioning sperm, which remains functional only two or three days, will be present in the reproductive tract in sufficient quantity when the female ovulates.

Choosing a Stud

Selecting the right stud requires thought and investigation. Ample leads can be found by visiting shows to study the cats being produced by today's studs and the people who own them; by reviewing yearbooks published by the cat federations; and by scrutinizing advertisements in various cat magazines and breed-association newsletters.

In all this deliberation, the novice breeder should be guided by three principles: the stud cat should live in an antiseptically clean cattery; he should come from a family or a line of cats that has crossed well with the female's line in the past; and he should be scrupulously efficient in producing those qualities the female lacks. If a female is light boned, for example, there is little chance of producing heavier bone in her kittens if the male she is bred to has produced only fine- to medium-boned kittens as a rule.

Genetics is so unpredictable that only the most carefully planned breedings have a better than random chance of producing top-quality kittens. In fact, the best that a breeder can do in any breeding (ad)venture is to minimize the chances for failure. To achieve this end, many breeders prefer using an older stud cat, one who is already a grandfather, because it is easier to judge a male's reproductive potential by looking at his children and their children than by looking at the honors he has won. Too many people scurry off to breed to the latest winner, who may have proven himself in the show ring but who has yet to prove himself otherwise — and whose success may be more a function of style than of substance. This year's glamour cats may develop into top producers one day, but for now it is more demonstrable that their fathers already have.

Contracts and Paperwork

Although they have little jurisdiction over a cat's genes, breeders can control the logistics of the mating process. No owner should send a female to a cattery to be bred unless the owner of that cattery is willing to provide a current health certificate for the stud cat in question and for any other cats with whom the female is likely to come into contact. What's more, owners should be wary of sending their females to catteries that do not request the same certification for incoming females.

The stud-service contract is another document that should accompany all breeding arrangements. This contract does not have to be complicated or lengthy, but it should declare the fee involved, the responsibilities of the stud owner while the female is in his or her care, the length of time the stud owner is willing to keep the female, and the boarding fee, if any, that the stud owner charges for feeding and housing visiting females. The stud-service contract also should stipulate what happens if the female is mated but does not conceive; if she conceives but loses her kittens prematurely after she returns home; if she has only one live kitten; and any other eventuality that the parties to the contract consider important enough to put in writing.

A stud-service contract, freely signed by two parties of sufficient age and mental capacity, is a legally binding document. Oral agreements are also legally binding, but cannot be supported without witnesses.

Before You Breed Your Cat

The antics of a cat in season, the plaintive vocal and postural entreaties, the sophisticated lady gone courtesan or clown—these are demonstrations that certify the breeder's license to dream, to cut the genetic deck in search of the ultimate draw.

But just as poker players often need jacks or better to open, breeders need to bring seriousness, responsibility, and purpose to the table before they set about producing kittens. Too many people use breeding to feed their competitive egos, to turn a fast buck, or to let their children observe the mystery of birth. But with millions of healthy, mixed-breed cats being destroyed annually for want of good homes—and with as many as 75,000 pure-bred cats winding up in shelters each year—the decision to bring more kittens into the world should not be made frivolously. Indeed, most people should not make, or even consider, this decision at all.

Everyone who produces kittens contributes, however indirectly, to the surplus-cat population because pedigreed kittens frequently are purchased by people who might have adopted a homeless kitten from a shelter instead. Yet few people who produce kittens contribute significantly to the improvement of their breeds. Competition in the show ring is intense. Thus, few breeders become overnight sensations. The laws of genetics are as fickle as they are immutable. Thus, few, if any, litters are filled with nothing but show-quality kittens. The economics of breeding are exacting. Thus, few people profit as much from raising kittens as they would for working the same number of hours at minimum wage.

People who do not add as much to a kitten's life as a kitten adds to theirs should not produce kittens. Nor should anyone produce kittens if he or she would not be willing to go live with the people to whom a kitten is being sold.

An ordinance passed in San Mateo County, California, in 1991 requires that breeders help persons who have bought kittens from them within the past year to find homes for those kittens if the buyers will not or cannot continue to keep the kittens. The ordinance further requires that if homes cannot be found for such kittens within six months, the breeders must assume responsibility for and possession of those kittens. Such an ordinance should be written on every breeder's heart.

Raising Scottish Folds

Identifying Pregnancy

Female cats normally ovulate 25 to 36 hours after mating successfully, but ovulation may not occur until 50 hours afterward. Thus, the earliest a female can conceive is the day following her first successful mating. Generally, a female pays tribute to mating success by screaming loudly, striking out at her suitor, rolling about madly, and grooming herself vigorously.

About three weeks later, a pregnant female's nipples begin to swell slightly and to turn rosy pink. By then, each kitten embryo she is carrying is barely ½ inch (1.3 cm) long. These embryos and their associated membranes can be detected through abdominal palpation between 17 and 25 days after conception. Ultrasonography, which identifies each kitten by means of reflected sound waves, can identify the amniotic sac enclosing a developing embryo 18 days after conception and is able to detect the fetus and fetal heartbeats after 25 days. Toward the end of the sixth week of pregnancy, the mineralized, opaque fetal skeleton is visible on abdominal radiographs. These help veterinarians to estimate the number of kittens a female is carrying and, because different bones become visible on radiographs at different stages of pregnancy, radiographs also can help to determine a litter's approximate age and delivery date for those breeders who are not certain when their females were bred.

Care During Pregnancy

Some cat owners, interpreting the winking lights on their queens' (females') underbellies as a call to action, begin to sprinkle vitamins, minerals, and all sorts of additives to their queens' meals. Or they begin overfeeding their queens. Such attentions are not necessary and may be counterproductive. For the first four weeks of your cat's pregnancy, groom her as usual, play with her as usual, and feed her as usual—as long as you are feeding a product that is 100 percent nutritionally complete and balanced for all stages of a cat's life. If you must give your cat something extra, make it extra attention.

Step up your queen's rations, in gradual increments, beginning with the fifth week of pregnancy. According to National Research Council estimates, pregnant queens need .45 ounces (13 g) of dry food per pound of body weight each day, .6 ounces (17 g) of semimoist food, or 1.4 ounces (40 g) of canned food. These amounts represent increases of 41 percent, 50 percent, and 40 percent, respectively, over normal feeding requirements. (See Daily Feeding Guidelines, page 00.)

If your 7-pound (3.2 kg) Scottish Fold queen was eating 7 ounces (200 g) of canned food daily, she ought to be eating 9.8 ounces (280 g) a day by the end of her pregnancy, having reached that quota gradually. Because the queen's abdomen becomes more crowded during pregnancy, distribute her food over three meals a day soon after you begin increasing her rations. If you notice that the dry-food bowl needs topping up more often than usual, measure the amount you set out there to prevent her from consuming more than the recommended .45 ounces (13 g) per pound each day. Queens that gain too much weight during pregnancy often have large kittens, poor muscle tone, fatty deposits that narrow the birth canal through which the fat kittens must pass, and difficult deliveries.

Just as overfeeding during pregnancy is counterproductive, so are overdoses of vitamins and minerals, unless a queen was bred accidentally before she had recovered from raising a previous litter or unless she is ill and your veterinarian has recommended supplementation. Excess calcium, phosphorous, and vitamin D can cause bone and kidney damage. Excess vitamin A can cause sterility and coat loss.

Finally, queens should not be exposed to teratogens during pregnancy. Defined as substances that disrupt normal embryonic development, teratogens include live-virus vaccines, excess doses of vitamin A, some steroids, and griseofulvin, an antidote for ringworm and fungus. These and other teratogenic substances are always potentially harmful to the developing embryo.

Preparing for Delivery

Gestation, the period between conception and birth, lasts, on average, 63 to 69 days after a female's initial successful mating. Sixty-five or 66 days is the usual duration, but viable kittens have been born between 59 and 71 days.

About the start of her last week of pregnancy, the queen begins investigating open closets, drawers, and the undersides of beds in search of a nesting place. From then on, she ought never to be left alone for more than a few minutes at a time.

Given the choice, most queens would spend the last several nights of pregnancy on their owners' beds. Indeed, that is where many cats prefer to spend their nights. If anyone objects to this arrangement, the queen should be installed in a double cage in her owner's bedroom. The bedroom door should be kept closed, and children and other pets should be kept at bay. With the queen close at hand, even the most comatose sleepers will be responsive to any unusual noises, ratting about in the cage, or signs of distress in the night.

Double cages can be purchased from companies that advertise in cat magazines, and sometimes they can be purchased from cat clubs that have surplus cages. Most double cages are roughly 22 inches (56 cm) deep and tall and 44 inches (112 cm) wide.

Provision the queen's cage with food, water, a litter pan, and a nesting box. The top or bottom half of a cat carrier or a modified cardboard box make a decent nest. If you use a cardboard box, leave three sides intact and cut the front side down so that a 4-inch-high strip (10 cm) is left at the bottom to prevent newborn kittens from crawling out. Spray the nesting box with a mild, nonammonia-based disinfectant and wipe it dry before placing it in the cage. Some breeders use cloth towels to line the nesting box, others use newspaper or paper towels.

Many breeders begin taking their females' temperatures morning and night with a rectal thermometer on day 58 after the first mating. A cat's temperature is normally 101.5°F (38°C) or thereabout. If the temperature drops to 98 or 99°F (36.7-37°C), kittens will most likely arrive within 12 hours. If the temperature rises two or three degrees above normal, call the vet at once.

As they begin to monitor a queen's temperature, owners of longhaired Folds should clip the hair around the anogenital area for sanitary reasons and around the nipples to make them more accessible to kittens. All owners should clip a queen's claws at this point, too.

Delivering Kittens

Temperature is not the only sign of impending delivery. Other signs include rapid breathing, deep purring, kneading with the paws, pacing, turning around in circles, frequent, somewhat anxious attention to the genital area, and passing the placental plug. This plug, a gelatinous stopper that forms at the cervix early during gestation to protect the uterus from external infection, is expelled when the cervix begins to relax in anticipation of delivery. The clear, stringy mucous that accompanies the passing of the plug may appear a few hours or a day or two before delivery.

As long as the queen emits a clear, odorless substance, her owner need not worry; but dark, green-tinted, odoriferous fluid is cause for concern. It may mean that a placenta has separated from the wall of the uterus and a kitten is in danger of dying from lack of oxygen—if it hasn't died already.

Labor begins with involuntary uterine contractions, which usually are preceded by rapid breathing, deep purring, and kneading with the paws. Not long after involuntary contractions have begun, a queen supplements them by contracting her abdominal muscles in an effort to deliver her first kitten. When abdominal contractions begin, the breeder should note the time carefully. If the first kitten does not appear within an hour, call the vet—and have a clean, towel-lined carrier ready.

As delivery begins, a dark, gray bubble emerges from the vagina. Once that bubble of new life appears, the clock should be reset to 30 minutes. If the queen cannot give birth to the kitten, either on her own or with help from her owner, during that time, call the veterinarian.

Kittens may present anteriorly, that is, come out head first, or posteriorly, tail first. In anterior presentations, if the queen does not deliver a kitten within five minutes after its head has emerged from her vaginal opening, remove the amniotic sac (or placental membrane) from around the kitten's face to prevent suffocation. The membrane should break and peel away easily if you rub the top of the kitten's skull gently with a clean finger or a piece of clean cloth. If the membrane breaks, peel it away from the kitten's face. If the membrane does not break, pinch it between your thumb and forefinger at the base of the kitten's skull and pull it away from the skull carefully. You may have to push the lips of the vulva back from the kitten's head in order to grasp the membrane at the base of the skull.

If another five minutes go by and the queen has not delivered the kitten on her own, you may be able to pull it free. You may also injure the kitten in the process. Injury is best avoided if you try to ease the kitten out rather than wrench it out.

After washing your hands, grasp the kitten between the thumb and forefinger of one hand as far behind the kitten's head as possible. If enough of the kitten is protruding, hook it between your index and middle fingers just behind its front legs. At the same time, support the queen's abdomen in the

other hand and push upward. Then pull the kitten gently downward. If the kitten still has not been delivered after 30 minutes, call the veterinarian.

In posterior presentations, time is more precious because you cannot remove the membrane from the kitten's face. What's more, if the umbilical cord is pinched inside the birth canal, cutting off the maternal blood supply to the kitten, the kitten will suffocate. If a kitten presents posteriorly and is not delivered within five minutes, begin trying to pull it out. If you are not successful after 10 to 15 minutes, call your vet.

Some breeders try to prompt delivery by giving their females a shot of oxytocin, a pituitary hormone that helps to stimulate uterine contractions. Do not attempt this at home without discussing the possibility with your veterinarian—and learning how to give a shot in advance. Oxytocin should never be administered before a kitten is visible in the vaginal opening. A queen can die of a ruptured uterus if she is given oxytocin before her cervix is fully dilated, and it is not easy for a nonprofessional to determine when dilation has occurred.

Once a kitten has been born, the queen should begin licking it vigorously to clean it and to remove the placental membrane. If she does not remove the membrane from the kitten's face at once, do it for her.

Healthy kittens usually move about in search of a nipple and may begin nursing within 15 minutes after birth. In the meantime, the queen will normally try to sever the umbilical cord with her teeth once she has passed the placenta, which usually occurs 5 to 15 minutes after she has delivered the kitten. Once the placenta has been expelled, the next kitten, if there is one, should appear within 10 to 90 minutes; but the interval between births is not as important as the queen's behavior. If she strains to deliver a kitten without success for an hour—or if a kitten appears in the vaginal opening and is not fully delivered within 30 minutes (or 10 to 15 minutes in the case of posterior presentations)—call the vet.

Raising Scottish Folds

Giving birth. The queen should begin licking the kitten vigorously to clean it and to remove the placental membrane.

If a newborn kitten is breathing with difficulty or does not appear to be breathing at all, and the queen has not expelled the placenta, fasten a hemostat on the umbilical cord about six inches (15 cm) from the kitten. Grasp the cord on the side of the hemostat closer to the mother and tug gently. If the mother does not expel the placenta at once, do not waste time with it. Cut the cord with sterile scissors on the mother's side of the hemostat, remove the hemostat, dip the severed end of the kitten's cord into a bottle of white iodine, and try to revive the kitten.

Place the kitten in a clean towel and then, holding the kitten in the towel between your hands, rub the kitten briskly to stimulate it and to help it to begin breathing. Hold the kitten in the palm of one hand, face up. Make sure the kitten's head is secure and immobile between your thumb and forefinger. Place your other palm over the kitten's abdomen with your forefinger over the kitten's heart.

Holding the kitten securely in both hands at about eye level, swing your hands downward abruptly for a distance of 3 or 4 feet (.9-1.2 m), pressing the rib cage over the kitten's heart with your forefinger as you do. Repeat two or three times. If the kitten does not begin breathing, hold its mouth open and blow gently into its mouth to resuscitate it. Swing the kitten downward two or three times more, blow into its mouth, swing, blow into its mouth, and swing again until the kitten

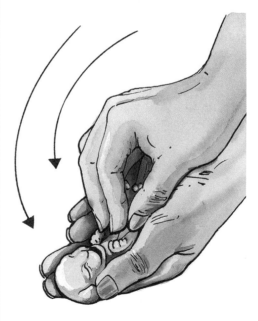

Reviving a fading kitten.

73

begins breathing or until it is obvious that the kitten is beyond reviving. Do not think about throwing in the towel until at least 30 minutes have passed.

Some breeders, if they cannot revive a kitten after five or ten minutes, dip it up to its neck into a bowl of very cool water and then into a bowl of very warm water in hope that the shock will kick start its heart. Breeders who have discussed the matter with a veterinarian beforehand sometimes put a drop of the respiratory stimulant Dopram-V under the kitten's tongue to activate breathing at this point.

If a weak kitten begins breathing on its own, place it in a small box that has a heating pad on the bottom and a towel over the pad. The temperature in the box should be 85°F (29°C). To maintain that temperature, you may have to put another towel loosely over the kitten, close the flaps of the box, and place a towel over the closed flaps. Give the kitten back to its mother when she has finished delivering her litter, but continue to monitor that kitten for the next two hours.

Some mothers chew each umbilical cord and eat every placenta compulsively, but after your queen has consumed two placentas, dispose of any others, or she may develop an upset stomach or diarrhea. If the queen shows little interest in umbilical cords or placentas, cut the cords five minutes or so after the kittens have been born, sterilize the severed ends of the cords that are attached to the kittens, and dispose of the afterbirths. Be sure all placentas are present and accounted for. A retained placenta can cause serious infection, may have to be removed surgically, and could mean that the breeder instead of the queen will be raising the litter.

After the last kitten has been delivered, the queen will heave a sigh of relief and settle in to nursing and fussing over her brood. As she does, inspect each kitten for signs of abnormalities such as cleft palates and umbilical hernias.

At this point, some breeders give their queens a shot of oxytocin to expel any placental debris retained during delivery. Check with your veterinarian in advance about the advisability of doing this.

Monitor the kittens and their mother for two hours after the last kitten has been born to make sure that all kittens are nursing normally and that the temperature in the kitten box is sufficient to prevent chilling. Kittens should begin nursing no later than two hours after they have been born. If a kitten appears too weak to nurse, you may have to tube feed it (see Supplemental Feeding below).

Maintain the temperature in the kitten box at 85°F (29°C) by putting a heating pad under the towel in the box if necessary. Kittens' homeostatic mechanisms, which regulate their body temperature, are not completely functional at birth. Normally an attentive queen's body heat will maintain kittens' temperatures at the normal 100 to 101°F (37–38°C). After two weeks, the temperature in the nesting box can be reduced to 80°F (26.7°C).

Neonatal Kitten Development

Kittens should begin nursing within two hours after being born. They nurse almost hourly for the first day or two. Indeed, they have only two primary modes, nursing and sleeping, which they execute in a 1:3 ratio.

On average, kittens weigh 3.1 to 3.9 ounces (88–110 g) at birth. They may not gain weight during their first 24 hours. They may even lose a few grams. After that, however, they should gain ½ ounce (15 g) a day during their first week, doubling their weight in that interval. If a kitten fails to gain weight during any 48-hour period in its first two weeks of life, or if a kitten begins to lose weight, call your veterinarian. By the time it is one month old, the average kitten should weigh between 14.1 ounces (400 g) and 15.9 ounces (450 g).

To support this growth, a lactating queen requires 1 ounce (29 g) of dry food or 1.3 ounces (37 g) of semimoist food or 3.3 ounces (94 g) of canned food per pound of body weight each day, depending on the number of kittens she is nursing, their size, and age. These amounts represent increases of 120 percent, 117 percent, and 136 percent respectively over the rations the queen was receiving at the end of pregnancy.

Supplemental Feeding

If a kitten is not nursing, if it seems to be crying more than it is nursing, or if it is not gaining weight as it should be, it most likely will benefit from supplemental feeding. Begin by taking the kitten's temperature with a rectal thermometer that has been lubricated with Vaseline or K-Y Jelly. If the kitten's temperature is below 97°F (36°C), feed it 2 cc's of warmed 98°F (36.7° C) dextrose solution. Below 97°F (36°C), enzymes in the kitten's stomach are not functioning well enough to digest milk. If the kitten's temperature is above 97°F (36°C), feed it 2 cc's of mother's milk replacer. You can obtain the dextrose solution, the mother's milk replacer, and the syringe with which to administer them from your vet a few days before your queen is due. Keep the dextrose solution, and the milk replacer once it has been opened, in the refrigerator.

Whether you feed dextrose or milk, the technique is the same. Put a towel on your lap, hold the kitten in one hand at a 45° angle to your lap, slide the end of the syringe gently between the kitten's lips, and push the plunger on the syringe a fraction of an inch to release some of the contents of the syringe into the kitten's mouth. Go slowly, pushing intermittently on the plunger as the kitten sucks on the syringe. Some kittens suck so vigorously they can move the plunger with little assistance from their owners. If the kitten is sucking avidly and then turns its head away, it is full.

Kittens whose temperatures are normal can be returned to their mothers after supplemental feeding, but they should be monitored carefully to be sure they are nursing adequately within an hour or so. If they are not, continue supplemental feeding

Feeding a kitten with a syringe.

every two hours around the clock until they begin nursing on their own.

Kittens whose temperatures are subnormal should be placed in an incubator and monitored every hour. As long as their temperatures remain below 97°F (36°C), keep feeding the dextrose solution. When the kitten's temperature rises above 97°F (36°C), feed it a milk replacer, then give it back to its mother. Watch the kitten every hour or so to see if it is nursing properly. If not, feed it 2 cc's of dextrose solution or milk replacer every two hours around the clock until it is able to nurse normally.

Kittens too weak to suck dextrose solution or milk from a syringe may have to be tube fed. Ask your veterinarian in advance to show you how to measure the length of tube, attached to a syringe, that needs to be inserted into the kitten's stomach.

Tube feeding, if not done properly, can cause lesions of the pharynx or stomach. If the tube is inserted incorrectly and food is introduced into the lungs, the kitten may choke and die. This method of feeding should be attempted, therefore, only as a last resort.

Raising Orphaned Kittens

Occasionally a queen will refuse to care for her kittens or she will be unable to care for them because she contracted an illness or has not recovered sufficiently from a Cesarean section to assume her maternal duties. In such circumstances, the owner must be prepared to hand-raise the litter until the queen recovers or the litter is old enough to eat on its own.

Orphaned kittens should be kept in an incubator at 85°F (29°C). Their temperatures should be checked every two hours around the clock for the first two or three days, and they should be fed 2 to 3 milliliters of warmed dextrose solution or milk replacer as their temperatures indicate for the first week.

If the kittens' temperatures are normal for a few days, you need not continue to take their temperatures before feeding. Intervals between feedings may be stretched to two and half hours during the second week and milk rations should be increased to 3 or 4 milliliters per feeding. During the third and fourth weeks, feed every three hours and give the kittens all the milk they want.

Toward the end of the kittens' third week, you should begin to wean them onto solid food. Begin with a porridge of baby cereal and milk replacer for a few days, then gradually add dry cat food that has been reduced to powder in a blender. At about four and a half or five weeks, switch to a mixture of canned cat food and whole dry cat food that has been soaked in milk. Finally, at about six weeks, switch to canned cat food or dry food alone.

For the first two or three weeks, you will have to stimulate kittens to eliminate before feeding them. Dip a section of wadded-up paper towel into a small bowl of warm water and rub each kitten's anogenital area softly. Wash the area with a clean paper towel after the kitten eliminates and then pat the kitten dry.

Kittens do not eliminate spontaneously until they are three weeks old. When they begin, provide them with a litter pan and show them how to use it. Place kittens in the pan as soon as they wake up from a nap or right after you have fed them. Take their front paws in each of your hands and scratch the litter gently. They will soon get the idea.

Because hand-raised kittens have not received maternal antibodies, ask your veterinarian if they should be vaccinated at eight weeks or if he or she recommends starting vaccinations, using killed vaccine, when the kittens are three to four weeks old.

If hand-raising kittens sounds like work, it is. During several sleep-deprived weeks your determination and self-discipline are all that stand between life and death for the kittens. But you decided to bring them into the world, so you are responsible for seeing them through it.

When you have hand-raised a litter successfully, the kittens' progress is a bountiful reward. What's more, the kittens you have nurtured faithfully will be among the best socialized, most people-oriented tykes you will ever see.

The Kitten Delivery List

1. the veterinarian's emergency number
2. a quantity of clean, soft cloths
3. a supply of clean towels
4. small hemostat (presterilized in boiling water)
5. scissors (presterilized in boiling water)
6. white iodine
7. aspirator
8. heating pad
9. small box
10. oxytocin (optional)
11. Dopram-V (optional)
12. several syringes
13. an eye dropper
14. a clean, towel-lined carrier
15. dextrose solution (refrigerated)
16. a can of commercial mother's milk replacer
17. coffee

Scottish Fold Genetics

From Mutations to Cat Breeds

The Scottish Fold's captivating ears are the work of a genetic mutation. Ordinarily nature transmits the genetic instructions that govern the inheritance of physical characteristics with the efficiency of a smoothly functioning telephone system. Every so often, however, the message gets scrambled and a caller winds up with a wrong number or an extra party on the line. In genetics, such random alterations in service are called mutations.

While the telephone company seeks to correct "mutations" and to restore normal service, cat breeders sometimes try to preserve a new characteristic that results from a mutation and to design a breed around it. The Cornish and the Devon rexes, the Manx, and the Scottish Fold are four examples of breeds that have been based on mutations: the curly coat in the Rexes, the lack of a tail in the Manx, and the distinctive ears on a Scottish Fold.

Some Basic Genetic Terms

Hereditary transactions are overseen by a group of large molecules called deoxyribonucleic acid (DNA). These molecules are arranged in tightly coiled strands called chromosomes. The nucleus of most body cells in the cat contains 38 chromosomes. Thirty-six of them are deployed in 18 matched pairs. Chromosomes that occur in matched pairs are also called autosomes. The two remaining chromosomes are called sex chromosomes because they determine a cat's gender.

A chromosome carries many genes, the coding units that transmit genetic instructions from one generation to the next. Each gene occupies a specific "address" (or site) on a chromosome. That address is called the gene's locus (plural, loci).

Although a gene always occupies the same locus on each member of an autosomal pair, that gene may occur in different forms called alleles. At the locus for ear structure in the cat, for example, there is either an allele that tells the ears to grow normally or an allele that tells them to do something different. Cats with normal ears have two normal-ear alleles—one at each of the ear-structure loci of an autosomal pair.

The Fold-ear Allele

A genetic mutation producing an allele that caused a cat's ears to fold forward and downward occurred in a barn cat born in Scotland in 1961. (See *The Scottish Fold Story*, page 11.) The first analysis of the nature and effects of that allele was conducted by Pat Turner, a British cat breeder. Turner began her inquiry in 1967 after she had obtained a fold-eared male from William and Mary Ross, the first Scottish Fold breeders of record. At first Turner bred that male to British Shorthairs. When she found that not all the offspring of a fold-eared-straight-eared mating develop folded ears, she also used some of those straight-eared offspring in her breeding program. Eventually she produced 76 kittens: 42 with folded ears and 34 with straight ears.

In 1969 Turner and Peter Dyte, a British geneticist, wrote an article for the *Carnivore Genetics Newsletter*, a journal published in the United States. They explained that the mutated allele causing folded ears is an autosomal dominant. Autosomal means that the allele occurs on an ordinary chromosome. Dominant means that if a kitten inherits one allele for folded ears and one allele for straight ears, that kitten will develop folded ears.

Their folded ears, which were smaller than the ears on straight-eared cats, were not the only unusual characteristic of the early Folds. Mary Ross had written that Susie, the first Scottish Fold, had a short, thick tail; and Turner reports that Denisla Snowdrift, the fourth-generation male she got from

Scottish Fold Genetics

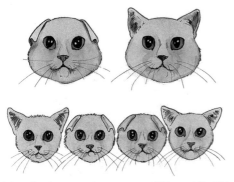

A breeding between a heterozygous, fold-eared Scottish Fold (top, left) and a homozygous, straight-eared cat (top, right) will produce two heterozygous Folds and two homozygous straight-eared cats (bottom).

the Rosses, had a short tail also and that his "hind legs moved stiffly and his limbs were thick."

Because Snowdrift's mother was a straight-eared British Shorthair, a breed with no history of folded ears, Snowdrift must have been a heterozygous Fold. (A cat that inherits two different alleles of a gene governing a particular trait is said to be heterozygous for that trait.) Indeed, most early Folds were heterozygotes because most were the products of matings between fold-eared and straight-eared cats.

In time, says Mary Ross, she and her husband "did breed one litter of Fold-to-Fold kittens," which contained a female with a short, thick tail and obviously deformed hind limbs. When the Rosses told Turner about this crippled kitten, she called Dr. Pat Scott, who worked at the Royal Free Hospital School of Medicine in London. Scott agreed to take the kitten, then about four months old, for observation. After a while, she gave the kitten to a veterinary surgeon named Oliphant Jackson, MRCVS, who was working toward a doctorate under Scott's direction. Jackson decided to breed several litters of fold-eared cats and to observe their development as part of his doctoral

studies. He was interested in Folds, Turner recalls, as a possible model for investigating dwarfism in humans.

The Jackson Report

In 1975, Jackson published the results of his observations in the *Bulletin of the Feline Advisory Bureau (BFAB)*. He had observed the effects of three kinds of breedings: (1) between two skeletally normal Folds, (2) between normal Folds and Folds with skeletal lesions, and (3) between Folds with skeletal lesions and normal cats with straight ears.

Breedings between two skeletally normal Folds produced 13 live kittens. Twelve developed folded ears. Four of those 12 were skeletally affected.

Breedings between normal Folds and Folds with lesions produced six live kittens. All developed folded ears. Two were skeletally affected.

Breedings between Folds with lesions and straight-eared cats produced nine live kittens. All developed folded ears. None were skeletally afflicted.

Jackson radiographed selected kittens "at regular intervals until the skeleton had fully matured." He found that skeletal lesions could be identified radiographically when kittens were 50 days old. The abnormal conditions that he observed among skeletally afflicted Folds included short, stumpy tails and deformities in the bones of the feet and lower legs. At six months, said Jackson, certain bones in the feet and lower legs of skeletally affected cats tend to fuse and a protrusion of abnormal bone and cartilage in the foot is easily recognized. Finally, the claws of skeletally affected kittens often become thick, like the beak on a parrot, because of the accumulation of dead layers of claw over the emerging new claw. This accumulation will curl downward and backward and grow into the paw pad if the nails are not clipped regularly.

Scottish Fold Genetics

Because the fold-ear allele is a simple dominant, said Jackson in his *BFAB* report, "it [is] easy to produce numerous fold-ear cats by breeding a fold-ear to a normal, prick-eared cat of any colour and not produce any skeletal abnormality." Yet because he was rightly concerned about the effect of Fold-to-Fold breedings, Jackson "on two occasions in 1974...had warned the Cat Fancy and the veterinary profession that a heritable osteodystrophy of the cat was associated with the fold-eared breed."

Jackson stopped short of saying that the Governing Council of the Cat Fancy (GCCF) in England ought to slam the registry shut on Scottish folds. He merely "suggested that their breeding should be limited." Perhaps he did not follow the comings and the goings and the goings-on in the Cat Fancy too closely, for GCCF had banned the registration and exhibition of Scottish Folds about three years earlier on the untenable grounds that Folds are more prone to ear disease than are other breeds and are more difficult to treat for ear problems.

Jackson had produced nothing but normal fold-eared kittens when he had bred crippled Folds to straight-eared cats, therefore he reasoned that heterozygous Folds (those inheriting one fold-ear allele and one straight-ear allele) are normal. Crippled Folds, he concluded, must be homozygous for the fold-ear allele. (A cat is homozygous for a certain trait if it inherits two similar alleles for that trait.)

Yet if homozygosity is alone responsible for skeletal defects, why did heterozygous Folds like Susie, Snowdrift, and others have noticeably short tails and, occasionally, mild thickening in the hind limbs? And why do some breeders continue to see short tails, mild skeletal problems, and a thick claw or two in a small, but stubborn percentage of kittens born from Fold-to-straight breedings today?

"Considering the Jackson data and the subsequent observations of Fold breeders," says John C. Fyfe, DVM, research assistant professor of medical genetics at the University of Pennsylvania School of Veterinary Medicine, "we should allow for the possibility that the genetic or the external environment may modify the action of the gene enough so that in a few cases heterozygosity may cause mild skeletal abnormalities. We should also allow for the possibility that in a few cases a cat could be carrying the fold allele but not have folded ears. Some breeders have observed that the ears of a few cats will straighten after being folded for a time. Such cats, though phenotypically straight eared, would be heterozygous Folds genotypically. (A cat's phenotype is its physical appearance. Its genotype is its genetic makeup.)

"These assumptions indicate another area of investigation: Can anyone show that the allele producing skeletal deformities is not the same one that makes the ears fold? No one has demonstrated that."

The occasional appearance of short tails and mild skeletal problems in heterozygous Folds has led Turner to conclude that "the effects of the fold-ear gene may not be just a simple folding of the ears but a syndrome, with complete penetrance for folded ears but incomplete penetrance for skeletal changes. I can't prove this," she says, "but I think it." (Penetrance, usually expressed as a percentage, is the frequency with which a gene produces its effect. For "complete penetrance" one may read "100 percent of the time.")

Fold-to-Fold Breeding

Though the abnormalities arising from Fold-to-Fold breedings are not life threatening, and the allele for folded ears is not lethal, Fold-to-Fold breedings are an imprudent strategy. Many observers believe that the osteodystrophy occurring in kittens from Fold-to-Fold breedings is not a pain-free condition.

"The bony proliferation of the foot and ankle bones causes inflammation and pain until such

Scottish Fold Genetics

time as the abnormal bones grow together and can no longer move relative to each other," says Fyfe. "At this stage pain may subside, or it may continue intermittently as the abnormal, and not very strong, bone suffers microfractures. Of course, the fusion of joints by dystrophic bone, whether pain is present or not, drastically reduces the normal range of joint motion and may inconvenience the cat."

If the potential of putting a cat at risk for a lifetime of discomfort were not sufficient cause to avoid Fold-to-Fold matings, the lack of profit from this dangerous investment would be. Unions between a heterozygous Fold and a straight-eared cat produce, on average, two Folds out of four kittens born. Unions between heterozygous Folds produce three Fold kittens, on average, out of every four kittens born. But one of those three kittens, again on average, is going to be homozygous, and hence crippled, and hence not showable.

Some people think they will profit from using a crippled Fold for breeding, especially if it is only slightly crippled and they are able to convince themselves that it is not in any pain, because homozygous Folds produce nothing but fold-eared kittens. Jackson demonstrated as much in his study. What's more, all nine kittens out of skeletally affected Folds and straight-eared cats in Jackson's study developed normally.

Setting aside judgments about the moral net worth of persons who would put an animal at risk deliberately, one must observe that if kittens with shortened tails and mild crippling in the hindquarters sometimes result when normal Folds are bred to straight-eared cats, who is to say such kittens will not occur—and will not occur more often—when crippled Folds are bred to straight ears? Most breeders who produce short-tailed kittens, even heterozygous ones, prefer to sell them as pets rather than risk using them for breeding. And many breeders believe that by using only normal-tailed Folds in Fold-to-straight breedings, the incidence of short-tailed, heterozygous kittens can be reduced to nearly zero.

Inbreeding

In addition to preaching against Fold-to-Fold matings, most Fold breeders advise against inbreeding, which is generally defined as father-daughter, mother-son, or brother-sister matings. Inbreeding is the most efficient way to produce kittens that are homozygous at various loci and are, therefore, more likely to pass on their inherited characteristics. (In breeder's parlance, this is known as "setting type.")

"You just can't do [inbreeding]," says one longtime Fold advocate. "Inbreeding may explain why people get problems from Fold-to-straight breedings occasionally. They've inbred, and even when they outcross to British or American shorthairs, they still get problems."

Fyfe does not believe that inbreeding, per se, between Fold-eared and straight-eared cats, or between two Folds, will intensify problems associated with the fold-ear gene. He points out, however, that inbreeding, because it results in a greater degree of homozygosity, is just as likely to allow deleterious recessive traits to express themselves as it is to lock in desirable traits. (A recessive trait does not become apparent unless an individual inherits two alleles for that trait.)

If, for example, a straight-eared female is bred to a close fold-eared relative and both cats carry a recessive gene for a metabolic disease like cystic fibrosis, their kittens are more likely to be affected by that disease than kittens born from that same straight-eared female and an unrelated Fold male. But fold-eared kittens produced by brother and sister or two other close relatives are no more at risk for developing Fold-related osteodystrophy than are fold-eared kittens produced by less closely related parents.

Straight-eared Folds

Persons who want to raise Scottish Folds generally start by looking for the best fold-eared female money and connections can buy. There is, however, another option: buying a top-quality, straight-eared female. This option has much to recommend it.

First, the waiting list for good-quality straight-eared females is shorter than the one for comparable fold-eared girls. Second, the price for a straight-eared female is lower, by at least one third, than the price of a comparable fold-eared girl. Third, a straight-eared female makes just as good a breeder as a fold-eared girl. Fourth, breeders are more likely to sell a good straight ear than a good Fold to a novice. Fifth, if your Fold girl's ears straighten up and stay there when she goes into season halfway to her grand championship, you will not feel as bad having bred her as you would feel if you had paid $1,200 for her.

Because the genetic background and the modifiers on which the fold-ear allele "lands" may influence the extent to which a cat's ears fold, persons looking for a straight-eared female would do well to select one that has a littermate or a parent with extremely tight ears. The straight-eared female may not have inherited the fold-ear allele, but she may have inherited the modifiers that facilitate a tighter degree of folding in the ears.

Breeding Strategies

Although Fold breeders with a light-boned cat would breed to a sturdy-boned cat to correct that situation and Fold breeders with a long-bodied cat would breed to a shorter-bodied cat, many of those same breeders insist there is no correlation between tightness of ears in parent and offspring. Folds with the tightest ears, these breeders tell you, will produce Folds with extremely loose ears and vice versa. These outcomes are certainly possible, but one has to wonder if this range of effects is unique to tightness of ears or if it is simply an instance of the law of errors at work: a law that applies to all heritable traits.

According to the law of errors, small errors occur more often than large ones; very large errors very seldom occur; as errors become progressively larger, they become less numerous; and negative errors occur about as often as positive errors (that is, the field goal will be wide to the left as often as it will be wide to the right).

But what has all this trial about errors got to do with breeding cats? Simply that most of the fold-eared kittens produced by a fold-eared cat will have ears that are a little more or a little less tight than their fold-eared parent's ears. Occasionally (about 5 percent of the time) a kitten will exhibit seriously tighter or looser ears than its fold-eared parent has, but just as very large errors seldom occur, very large deviations from parental type seldom occur, either.

Though he has not bred enough kittens to test the theory, the author presumes that a tight-eared Fold male bred to a hundred females will produce more tight-eared kittens than a loose-eared Fold male who breeds those same one hundred females. Given the choice between two males equal in all significant respects but tightness of ears, only an optimist would select the one with the looser ears.

When Folded Ears Go Straight

No one is certain why some Folds' ears do not remain folded throughout life. Often, when females go into season, get pregnant, or simply get older, their ears rise as if to salute these signal occasions. The author once owned a Fold girl whose right ear rose to celebrate bringing home fungus behind that ear from a show. Within days, the ear stood virtually straight while the other remained folded.

There are probably several causes that lead to these reversals of fortune. Whatever the causes might be, some observers believe that their immediate effect is the production of edema—an excess accumulation of fluid in the tissue of a cat's ears.

Scottish Fold Genetics

As the fluid builds up, the cat's ears go up, and the owner's spirits go down.

Sometimes flyaway ears return to their original nesting sites. The fungus-inspired straight ear gradually returned three or four weeks later to about 90 percent of its former, tightly folded splendor. Other times, flyaway ears stay virtually straight, rendering a cat unshowable. Because erstwhile Folds are still Folds genotypically, they should not be bred to other fold-eared cats.

Blood Types

Fold-to-Fold matings are not the only must to avoid for Scottish Fold breeders. Persons working with Folds should also avoid breeding a female with type B blood to a male with type A blood. Such marriages produce kittens at risk for neonatal isoerythrolysis (NI), an often fatal condition affecting kittens with type A blood that are born to females with type B blood. (Because type A cats have weak anti-B alloantibodies, type B kittens born to type A mothers are not at risk for NI.)

When NI strikes, the red blood cells of the type A kittens are destroyed by anti-A antibodies that those kittens have absorbed from the colostrum of their type B mothers. (Colostrum is the fluid, rich in protein and immune factors, that is secreted by the mammary glands during the first few days of lactation.)

The allele for type A blood is completely dominant over the allele for type B. Thus, if a type B female is bred to a type A male, half the kittens will have type A blood if the male is heterozygous for type A, and all the kittens will have type A blood if the male is homozygous for type A.

Not every type A kitten born to a type B mother will be challenged by NI, nor will every challenged kitten perish, but the mortality rate is high enough to warrant blood typing before breeding. Owners seeking to determine the blood type of their cats should ask their veterinarians if they have or know where to acquire blood-typing kits, which were expected to be available commercially by the fall of 1992. If veterinarians do not have such kits and do not know where to obtain them, breeders should ask their vets for the number of the nearest veterinary college and inquire there.

Determining blood type before breeding is especially important to Fold owners because 18 percent of all Scottish Folds have type B blood. There is roughly a one-in-five chance, therefore, that a Fold female is type B and a four-in-five chance that she will be bred to a type A Fold male. The combined probability of these events is about one in six. Thus, one out of every six breedings between an untyped Fold female and an untyped Fold male will produce kittens at risk for NI.

The allowable outcrosses for Scottish Folds, the British and American shorthairs, have type B frequencies of 40-plus and near-0 percent, respectively. There is, accordingly, about a one in eight chance that an untyped Fold female bred to an untyped British male will produce type A kittens at risk for NI, and a one in five chance that an untyped Fold girl bred to an untyped American Shorthair male will produce type A kittens at risk for NI.

Until recently, practicing veterinarians paid little attention to feline blood type. Anemic cats received transfusions routinely without much medical concern over the blood types of donor and recipient because the risk of encountering significant transfusion reactions was considered negligible. It is not. Consequently, all cats should be blood typed in case they ever need a transfusion.

Type A cats that receive a transfusion of type B blood may not exhibit obvious signs of illness, but because red blood cells are short lived following these transfusions, the transfusions are ineffective. When type B cats are transfused with type A blood (the kind most commonly supplied by donor cats), the A red cells do not live more than a few hours, if that. Such A-type-to-B-type transfusions may also result in restlessness, depression, spontaneous urination, seizures, and death.

Useful Reading and Addresses

Books

Behrend, Katrin and Monika Wegler. *The Complete Book of Cat Care*. Hauppauge, New York: Barron's, 1984.

Muller, Ulrike. *New Cat Handbook: Everything About the Care, Nutrition, Diseases, and Breeding of Cats*. Hauppauge, New York: Barron's, 1984.

Natoli, Eugenia. *Cats of the World*. New York: Crescent Books, 1987.

Robinson, Roy. *Genetics for Cat Breeders*. 2nd ed. Oxford: Pergamon Press, 1977.

Siegal, Mordecai, ed. *The Cornell Book of Cats*. New York: Villard Books, 1990.

Taylor, David. *The Ultimate Cat Book*. New York: Simon and Schuster, 1989.

Turner, Dennis C., and Patrick Bateson, eds. *The Domestic Cat: The Biology of its Behavior*. Cambridge, England: Cambridge University Press, 1988.

Wilson, Meredith. *Cat Breeding and Showing*. New York: A.S. Barnes & Company, 1972.

Wood, Philip, and Desmond Morris (editor). *A Passion for Cats*. London: Trafalgar Square, 1989.

Wright, Michael, and Sally Walters, eds. *The Book of the Cat*. New York: Summit Books, 1980.

Cat Magazines

Cats
2750-A South Rigewood Avenue
South Daytona, FL 32119

Cat Fancy
P.O. Box 6050
Mission Viejo, CA 92690

Cat Registries

The American Cat Association, Inc.
8101 Katherine Avenue
Panorama City, CA 91402
(818) 782-6080

American Cat Fanciers Association, Inc.
P.O. Box 203
Point Lookout, MO 65726
(417) 334-5430

Canadian Cat Association
83 Kennedy Road South
Unit 1805
Brampton, Ontario
Canada L6W 3P3
(416) 459-1481

The Cat Fanciers' Association, Inc.
P.O. Box 1005
Manasquan, NJ 08738-1005
(908) 528-9797

The Cat Fanciers' Federation, Inc.
9509 Montgomery Road
Cincinnati, OH 45242
(513) 984-1841

The International Cat Association, Inc.
P.O. Box 2684
Harlingen, TX 78551
(512) 428-8046

Feline Health and Welfare Organizations

American Humane Association
P.O. Box 1266
Denver, CO 80201
(303) 695-0811

American Society for the Prevention of Cruelty to
   Animals
   441 East 92nd Street
   New York, NY 10128
   (212) 876-7700
The Delta Society
   Century Building, Suite 303
   321 Burnett Avenue, South
   Renton, WA 98055
   (206) 226-7357
Friends of Animals
   P.O. Box 1244
   Norwalk, CT 06856
   For information about FOAs low-cost, neuter-
   ing-and-spaying program call:
   (800) 631-2212

The Fund for Animals
   200 W. 57th Street
   New York, NY 10019
   (212) 246-2096
Humane Society of the United States
   2100 L Street, NW
   Washington, DC 20037
   (202) 452-1100
Morris Animal Foundation
   45 Inverness Drive, East
   Englewood, CO 80112-5480
   (800) 243-2345

Index

Inherited immunity, 47
Internal parasites, 47, 49
International Scottish Fold Association (ISFA), 14
Iodine, 39, 73, 76
Iron, 39
Itching, 49

Jackson, Oliphant MRCVS, 78–80
report, 78

Kidney stones, 39
Kitten(s), 12, 16–22, 24, 26, 29, 32, 33, 41, 48, 49, 57, 61, 69, 78, 81, 82
body, 19
eyes, 19
fails to gain weight, 74
first week of life, 74, 76
homeostatic mechanisms, 74
neonatal development, 74
nesting box, 71, 74
nursing, 72, 74, 75
poorly adjusted, 18
proper age for leaving their mothers, 19
raising orphans, 75
resuscitating, 73
selecting a healthy kitten, 16, 19
short-tailed, 80
shy kittens, 19
weaning, 76
weight at birth, 74
weight loss, 74

Lack of energy, 44
See also Illness, signs of
Lack of interest in food, 43
See also Illness, signs of
Lactating, 41, 74
Larvae, 49
Lethargy, 44
See also Illness, signs of
Lice, 49
Liquids, 39
Lite food, 42
Litter pan, 23, 25, 26, 29–31, 51, 59, 60, 71, 76
Litter pan liners, 23
Litter scoop, 23, 59
Litter training, 20, 26
Liver, raw, 39
Locus (loci), 77, 80
Longhaired kittens, 12, 15
Longhair gene, 12, 15
Longhair(s), 12, 15, 32
Lordosis posture, 66

Magnesium, 39
Manganese, 39
Meat, raw, 39, 42
Melatonin, 65
Metestrus, 65
Miacids, 7
Mineral oil, 32, 35, 37
Minerals, 38–40, 42, 70
Mites:
body 49
ear, 19
Molybdenum, 39

Mother's milk replacer, 75, 76
Mutations, 13, 77

Nematodes, 49
Neonatal isoerythrolysis, 82
Neutering, proper age for, 16
Niacin, need for, 39
Nickel, 39
Nursing a sick cat, 51

Osteodystrophy, 19, 79, 80
Outcross, 14, 80, 82
nonsanctioned, use of, 15
Overweight, signs of, 42
Ovulate, 67, 68, 70
Ovulation, 67, 68, 70
Oxytocin, 72, 74, 76

Pale gums, 19, 44, 50
See also Illness, signs of
Papers, 15, 20–22
Parasiticidal dips, 49
Pets, introducing others to new cat, 29, 67
Pet sitters, 31
Phenotype, 79
Phosphorus, 39, 42
Pill guns, 52
Pilling, 52
Pineal gland, 65
Placenta, 71–74
Placental membrane, 72

Placental plug, 71
Plaque, 50
Poisonous plants, 25
Posterior presentations, 72
Potassium, 39
Pregnancy, 70
care during, 70
confinement during, 29
identifying by abdominal palpation, 70
identifying by abdominal radiographs, 70
identifying by taking female's temperature, 71
identifying by ultrasonography, 70
increasing food during, 70
involuntary contractions, beginning, 72
overfeeding during, 70
Pregnant, 39, 41, 49, 70, 81
Pregnant and lactating cats, 41
Preventive health care, 47
Proestrus, 65, 66
Protein, 38–40, 82
Protozoa, 49
Pus, 44

Rabies vaccine, 48
Rapid breathing, 44, 71, 72
See also Illness, signs of